THE IMPOSSIBLE PEOPLE

A History Natural and Unnatural of Beings Terrible and Wonderful

BY GEORGESS McHARGUE
illustrated by Frank Bozzo

Through the millennia, every culture has developed its own mythologies, each with a wealth of mythological, "impossible," people. Giants, Trolls, Witches, Pixies, Demons, Mermaids—the forms are as varied as the human imagination, and yet, to sometimes surprising extent, many of the basic ideas are universal.

With wit and erudition, Georgess McHargue here offers a marvelous compendium of mythological beings. Frank Bozzo has unleashed his imagination to picture them in all their gothic splendor. American and European folklore are the author's main fields of research, but pertinent and exotic examples range as far as the Zambesi and the Himalayas. She analyzes and describes the chief mythological "people," noting the curious backward evolution—from god to whimsey—that characterizes many. There are also practical speculations on the possible origins of these persistent imaginary beings. The whole is studded with dramatic and amusing anecdotes—sure to please all young readers, from budding sociologists to those who simply love a good tale.

THE
IMPOSSIBLE
PEOPLE

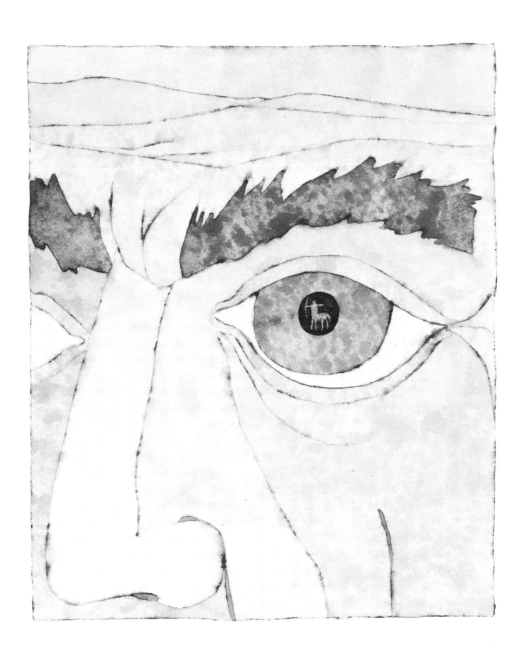

THE IMPOSSIBLE PEOPLE

A History Natural and Unnatural
of Beings Terrible and Wonderful

BY GEORGESS McHARGUE

illustrated by Frank Bozzo

HOLT, RINEHART AND WINSTON—NEW YORK CHICAGO SAN FRANCISCO

ISBN : 0-03-080237-7 (Trade)
ISBN : 0-03-080238-5 (HLE)
Library of Congress Catalog Card Number : 75-150033
Printed in the United States of America
Designed by Susan Mann
First Edition

This one is for John and Alice,
who are interested in monsters
and even people.

CONTENTS

INTRODUCTION   ix

I BIG PEOPLE   1

II THE FAERY FOLK   27

III LITTLE PEOPLE   47

IV WORKERS OF EVIL—
AND A FEW GOOD SPIRITS   74

V THE HALFWAY PEOPLE   105

VI THE PEOPLE OF THE SEA   135

BIBLIOGRAPHY   159

INDEX   163

INTRODUCTION

ONE OF THE THINGS that happened when man became different from the animals was that he *knew* that he was different. At some time in the long course of evolution this creature man began to look at himself and the rest of the world. He looked, and wondered why, and tried to explain what he saw, and he has been doing so ever since.

To those early men their planet must have been a mysterious place, full of surprises. And perhaps because man has always thought of *himself* as the most fascinating, powerful, wonderful being in creation, he naturally saw the forces around him as man-like. If the thunder roared it was the battle cry of some huge and horrifying tribe called Giants. If the people fell ill it was the unseen work of evil Demons. If a man drowned it was because a Water Spirit had pulled him under and held him, embracing him almost as a woman would.

That appears to be one way in which the Impossible People, the subjects of this book, were born. Later as man's imagination continued to work on his creations, they were changed in many ways. The most powerful among them came to be called gods, but in general we will not be concerned with gods here. Instead, we will look at the many kinds of imaginary beings who have held a less exalted place in man's mind.

The Impossible People were once thought to be as real as—and sometimes more real than—the folk who lived on the other side of the mountains or the ocean. After all, what forest-dwelling hunter of ancient Europe would have believed, at first hearing, a tale about the civilized men of northeastern Africa, with their mighty temples and pyramid-shaped tombs, their writing and sculpture and astronomy?

This brings us to the second major influence on the kind of thought that produced the Impossible People—the wonderful variety to be found in the natural world and in man's own cultures, behavior, and appearance. For example, it is quite within the normal range of things for human beings to vary in size from four feet, ten inches, to six feet, six; in color from pale pinkish tan to blackish brown; in weight from eighty-five pounds to two-hundred-fifty pounds. Likewise, different groups of men vary startlingly from each other in clothing and habits. In southern lands an Eskimo might be mistaken for a being covered in his own shaggy pelt instead of a man wearing sealskins. And among people who had never seen a horse, the first sight of a man riding might have started a legend about a strange being who was half man and half beast.

Well then, if men can differ so much from each other in these ways, why not in others? If there have been men who lived in caves and forests, grass huts and stone palaces, why not men who live in the air or under the sea? If man can light fires or harness the wind to propel his ships, why can't he move mountains, make himself invisible, run about in animal shape? Ideas like these are part of the way the human mind works, and it seems clear that there has never been a tribe or nation whose myths and folklore did not contain references to unpredictable, not-quite-human beings who could do marvelous things.

So men created myths and folktales. We still read and study those ancient stories today, and it is only reasonable to ask why. The story parts of myths are repetitive and the details don't usually make much sense to a modern reader. Hero-wins-maiden-by-killing-Dragon, world-is-created, despised-child-finds-fame-and-fortune, mysterious-prophecy-fulfilled, so run some of the most often repeated plots. Myths can be both dull and puzzling *until* it is clear what is really going on. The people who study such things have found that today's myth is sometimes yesterday's fact, although not in the literal sense. Many tales, of all peoples, hand down in disguised or distorted ways information about religious development, cultural changes, magical formulas, and events of the ancient past. This may be the case even when the meaning of the myth has been forgotten by those who tell it. The Greek story-poem of the Trojan War was thought to be a mere fiction until the nineteenth century, when a businessman named Heinrich Schliemann decided to take it literally and found the three-thousand-year-old city of Troy just where the poem said he would.

For this reason it is important to be sure that the myths and folklore we study are "genuine," that is, that they have really been handed down from former times and are not stories invented by modern writers, no matter how interesting the latter may be. Mythical beings are not "just made up," nor are they childish. They were once alive in the same way that all ideas are alive as long as they are believed—for it is not necessarily the facts but more often what is *believed* to be the truth that influences man's fears and dreams and actions.

I
BIG PEOPLE

There were giants in the earth
in those days.

—Genesis 6:4.
King James Bible

WHAT IS A GIANT? There are many answers, of course, but perhaps the best is that a Giant is the big man everybody is afraid of. He is the loud-voiced bully who steals your possessions and dares you to do something about it. He's the muscleman who takes over the town and runs things his way. He's the bigger boy who kicks over your sand fort. In short, he's the heavyweight champion of the world against whom no mere human being has a chance.

This idea of the big guy who can beat you up is so universal that there is hardly a place or people or period in history that does not have its tales of Giants and their equally fearsome cousins such as Ogres, Titans, Cyclopes, and Trolls.

In the mythologies of western Europe and elsewhere Giants are

1

thought of as a separate race of beings who existed before men, at the dawn of time. Greek myths of the creation of the world say that the children of the first couple, the earth-mother Gaea and the sky-father Uranus, were all Giants of one sort or another. First came the twelve Titans; then the three one-eyed Cyclopes, whose names show they represented various features of the thunderstorm; and last were the Hecatoncheires or "Hundred-handed Ones," who were also embodiments of the tumultuous forces of nature. The history of the Titans is complex, for later when there were wars among the gods some fought on one side, some on the other. In the end, the new gods who had won the mastery of the world were forced to imprison the Titans in order to restrain their terrible power. Now they are said to be chained at the roots of the world, but their rebellious stirrings still cause earthquakes and tidal waves.

On the whole the Giants of the Teutonic myths (those of Germany and Scandinavia) were quite similar to their counterparts in ancient Greece. Like the Titans, the Jotuns, as they were called, appeared on earth before there were any men. And because mythology reflects the world of the people who made it, the forces represented by the Teutonic Giants were those of northern Europe. The name Jotun means Devourer, and the Jotuns were also called Frost Giants since in those icebound mountains and forests the cold was surely man's most deadly enemy. It was the Jotuns' voices that roared in the thunder and in the breaking-up of icebergs, they who sent the hail to flatten the harvests, they whose strength was the strangling grip of winter itself.

Like the Greek gods, the Teutonic gods of the sky also had to conquer the Jotuns before they could rule. After a terrible battle, it was said, the gods killed Ymir, the father of all the Jotuns, and banished his

2

Big People

huge brood to the ice floes at the edge of the world. There in the Jotun-heim, or "Home of the Jotuns," they skulked angrily, waiting for a chance to take their revenge on the gods.

It was primarily in these myths about the Titans and Jotuns that the Giants of European folklore had their beginning. From the realm of religion they found their way into folklore, where they have remained ever since. The history of beliefs and ideas shows this change to be a common one. When one religion is replaced by another, as the pagan Greek and Teutonic systems were replaced by Christianity, figures from the ancient myths often remain in the people's imagination. They be-come subjects for songs and tales which serve at least partly for enter-tainment but which also keep alive the ideas of past times, though the tales may be much changed as they are handed down through the generations.

In the course of time, as the beings out of myth become more fa-miliar and less awe-inspiring, the tales come to say more and more about their habits and customs until we can feel we know their subjects—in this case the Giants—almost as well as we know our neighbors.

From all of the tales it is clear that Giants are not considered very civilized. Like ordinary human beings, they have wives and children and homes or even castles, but their ways and possessions are rough and clumsy. They may own great hoards of treasures, like the singing harp of the Giant who lived at the top of Jack's beanstalk, but such objects have almost always been stolen. After all, Giants are big enough to take anything they want.

Seldom does a Giant know anything about the skilled arts and professions. Even Giants' swords (when they use swords instead of

4

heavy, nail-studded clubs) are made for them by the Dwarfs (see Chapter III). The only exceptions to this rule are the special group of Giants who are the helpers of the Greek god Hephaistos, the supreme blacksmith, inventor, and iron-worker.

Giantesses, on the other hand, do seem to have one skill, although it is a gruesome and unusual one. They bake bread out of meal made from ground-up human bones, if we can believe the well-known rhyme ending, "Be he live or be he dead, I'll grind his bones to make my bread."

There is, however, at least one Giant who seems to have been a thoroughly nice fellow, although you would have had to travel to the coast of Somerset in England to meet him. The people thereabouts say that a Giant once came up to the town of Grabbist from somewhere down in Cornwall, and naturally nobody was very pleased to see him. However, this Giant seemed to be harmless and even anxious to make friends and gradually folk began to lose their suspicions. One day a terrific storm came up while the Giant was out fishing, standing about knee-deep in three or four fathoms of water. The gale didn't bother the Giant much, of course, but it caught the fishing boat "Dorcas Jane" on a lee shore and threatened to wreck her. As soon as the Giant saw the vessel was in trouble he picked her up out of the water, crew and all, and set her down safe in the nearest harbor. After that the people along that bit of coast became quite fond of the Giant. He used to come up by the town of Dunster to wash his feet in the river, and when he'd wave to his friends on shore, there was all the week's washing dried in one puff of wind.

Nevertheless, taken all together, Giants are a bad lot. Their crimes range from murder and cannibalism—though the latter is more usually

a trait of Ogres—to wholesale theft of food and livestock for their huge stomachs or wholesale destruction of the countryside if they are annoyed. It is rare to find a Giant as amiable as the Grabbist Giant in genuine folklore.

In view of the Giant's size and strength it is very lucky that they have one other major trait—they are not terribly bright. Though a Giant may be killed in a fair fight, it is usually better to try to outwit him. There is, for example, the tale of a Giant who had quarreled with the mayor of Shrewsbury, in England. In a fit of pique the Giant decided to drown the mayor's town by dropping huge rocks into the nearby Severn River until it overflowed its banks. Accordingly, the Giant set out for Shrewsbury one morning with a sack of tremendous boulders on his back. As he was going along the Giant met a cobbler who was coming from Shrewsbury with a load of shoes to mend. "What on earth are you doing with that great bag of rocks?" asked the cobbler. The Giant told him what he had in mind and inquired how much farther the town was, for the stones were getting heavy. "My, my," said the quick-thinking cobbler, regretfully. "You do have a long way to go, poor fellow. Why just look at all the shoes I've worn out on my way here from Shrewsbury." The Giant, of course, was convinced that the trip was too long to bother with, and the town was saved.

Wiping out a whole town is a typical way for a Giant to resolve a personal matter. Like his body, a Giant's anger is oversize.

One of the best tales of a slow-witted Giant is a very ancient one. It comes from the great Homeric epic poem *The Odyssey* and concerns the hero Odysseus and the Cyclops Polyphemus.

The Cyclopians whom Odysseus encountered are very typical

Giants except that they have only one eye, and that in the middle of their foreheads. They are not the same as the brothers of the Titans referred to earlier. In fact, the poem is very specific about their way of life. Odysseus calls them "a violent and lawless tribe" and says that they do not plant crops, build ships, or hold parliaments like the Greeks. Instead, they live in caves, where "each one lays down the laws for his wife and children, and no one cares for his neighbors." Polyphemus himself is "a wonderful monster, not like a mortal man who eats bread, but rather like a mountain peak with trees on the top standing up alone in the highlands." It would be hard to find a better description of Giants in general.

In the story, Odysseus and his crew have been shipwrecked on the island of the Cyclopians, and they take refuge in the huge cave of Polyphemus. Instead of helping the travelers, however, the Cyclops first imprisons them in the cave and then eats two of them alive. It is clear that the same fate waits for the rest unless they can escape. Fearfully, the men creep up on the Giant when he is asleep and put out his single eye with a sharp wooden stake. (They can't kill him outright because they know they could never move the enormous boulder that blocks the cave entrance.) But the Giant, blind and raging, calls out to the other Cyclopians for help, and it is then that Odysseus' cleverness becomes apparent. He has told Polyphemus that his name is Nemo, which means No-man. Thus when the other Giants hear Polyphemus' cries they call to him, asking whether he has been attacked. "No-man is killing me," roars the Giant. At that the others go back to sleep, grumbling at Polyphemus for having waked them, and Odysseus and his friends are able to escape, though not without further adventures.

Big People

Especially in the British Isles, Giants are often shown as rather cowardly as well as thick-headed. One tale hints that that was because, for all their strength, the Giants came to realize that they were at a disadvantage with those clever little human beings. There is a rather touching English story about a Giant child who peeped around a mountain one day and saw a farmer and his team plowing in the next valley. Running to her mother, the young one begged to be allowed to pick up the fascinating toy and bring it home to play with. The Giantess, however, wisely refused and warned her child to stay away from human beings. "They would drive us out," she explained; and maybe they did, for there are no Giants in England now.

Although Giants seem to have had a particular fondness for northern Europe, that is by no means the only place where tales about them are found. Among the Iroquois of North America, for instance, the Giants were described as powerful Magicians and great hunters. Unlike men, however, they did not know how to use the bow and arrow. Instead, their weapons were huge trees that they tore up by the roots. One of the chief Iroquois Giants was Ga-oh, who commanded the winds. He and his followers were much feared because, like the European Giants, they sometimes made a meal of human flesh.

On the other hand, Asian Giants were much more like the Titans and Jotuns in representing forces of nature. The popular Brahmanic mythology of India tells of the Maruts, immensely powerful sons of the god Rudra, Prince of Demons. The Maruts are unruly beings who go striding about the heavens and the earth with equal disregard. They hustle the clouds down the sky, flatten forests, and make the mountains shake, showing again the Giants' connection with bad weather.

Among the Giants found in the incredibly complicated mythology of China are the two assistants of the god of cattle-breeding. Their names are translated as The King of Oxen and The Transcendant Pig, and they are really more accurately described as the *ghosts* of Giants, because they became protectors of livestock only after spending lives of typically gigantic destructiveness. The King of Oxen is reputed to have terrified his enemies with his enormous horns and buffalo's ears, while The Transcendant Pig once had the unspeakable audacity to swallow a nephew of the Emperor of Heaven. Now, however, it is said they have been tamed and made into immortals.

That a Giant's destructive power can be leashed and used for good in this way is shown very clearly in the central European Jewish stories about the Golem. The Golem was a sort of homemade Giant. Although the practice was believed to be forbidden, or at least dangerous, many tales of the construction of a Golem were told among the Jews during the late medieval period.

To create a Golem one had to be familiar with the secret magical formulas contained in the Jewish books of lore, particularly the Cabala. The maker molded a figure out of "lifeless, shapeless matter" and then breathed life into it with the aid of the correct mystical procedures. The Rabbi Elijah of Chelm was supposed to have made a Golem that sounds very much like Frankenstein's Monster and had to be destroyed when it got out of control.

In form the Golem was exactly like a man except that he had great size and strength and lacked the power of speech. Perhaps the most famous story of the Golem is one told of sixteenth-century Prague. At that time the Jews of Poland (of which Prague was then a part) were

10

11

being unjustly persecuted by certain people who believed the Jews were murdering non-Jewish children in order to use their blood for religious rituals. Against this evil and untrue accusation the Jews of Prague found themselves helpless and they began to fear for their lives. In particular, the good Rabbi Yehuda Leow was concerned for the safety of his people, and he determined to take desperate measures in their defense. One dark night he repeated the magic formulas over a giant figure he had fashioned from the mud of the Moldau River. Brought to life, the Golem followed the Rabbi home, where the good man explained to his wife and neighbors that the huge fellow was a mute whom he had befriended.

Thereafter the Golem, on the Rabbi's instructions, patrolled the wall around the Ghetto every night. Eventually the watch was successful, and a man was caught trying to plant incriminating evidence in the house of a Jewish citizen. The arrest enabled Rabbi Leow to convince the King that the Jews were innocent of any crime. Once again, the people felt safe. On that night, exactly a year after he had made the Golem, the Rabbi led his creation up to the attic above the synagogue, where he put him to sleep on the floor, covered with sacks. The legend says that the Golem may rise up to help the Jews of Prague again, if ever he is needed.

We have seen that as tales have it Giants are usually dangerous but may sometimes have their good side. The same cannot be said for Ogres. On the average, Ogres are probably a bit smaller than Giants. That is little enough compensation for the fact that their only known occupation is to hunt down and eat human beings. They are also brutish and ugly. While Giants are said to look like anyone else except for their size and a certain shagginess, Ogres have flat faces, receding foreheads, heavy brows, piggy eyes, splayed noses, stooping shoulders, long arms, and sometimes pointed teeth. Though they have no beards they are very hairy over the rest of their bodies. They live in caves or filthy hovels and have personal habits that would be a credit to a sewer rat or hyena. They are not quite so stupid as Giants and frequently lure the unwary into their cooking pots by guile. However, one would not call them bright, and it is interesting to learn from one story that Ogres can only count up to five.

While the wives of Giants are most often stay-at-homes, this is not so with Ogres. In fact, Ogresses are some of the most horrible beings you could ever hope *not* to meet, making their male relatives seem quite charming by contrast.

Grendel and Grendel's Mother, two of the world's best known monsters, are probably to be classed as Ogres, although not everyone is agreed on this point. These antagonists of the Anglo-Saxon hero Beowulf are surely the most fearsome mother-and-son team in literature, and their man-eating habits, coupled with their monstrous but decidedly human-like forms, seem to point to Ogreish blood, even though some scholars have held that Grendel's Mother was a Hag or that they were both Water Demons.

Whatever Grendel was, he must have been quite large enough for an Ogre, for when we first meet him in the pages of the epic *Beowulf* he had broken into the great feasting hall of King Hrothgar and killed thirty men, whose bodies he then carried back to his lair. "Death and Grendel's great teeth came together, snapping life shut." Collecting the scattered information in the poem, we learn that Grendel lived in a

13

marsh, that his eyes "gleamed in darkness, burned with a gruesome light," that he had claws, and that his hide was made as tough as armor by magic.

Yet though the monster was invulnerable to the sword (and didn't use one himself) he met his match in Beowulf, who vowed to end Grendel's reign of terror and wounded him mortally in a wrestling match. But that is not the end of the story, for Grendel, like a good son, had been supporting his old mother at home in the marsh, bringing her human flesh to eat. Now the Ogress rushed out of her underwater lair, greedy both for man's meat and for revenge. Like Grendel she made it a practice to steal up on sleeping warriors and tear them to death, sometimes eating as many as fifteen on the spot. It was necessary for Beowulf to pursue her back to her stinking underwater home. When the hero at last tracked Grendel's Mother to her shining hall beneath the water, he saw there a magical Giant's sword with which he was finally able to kill the Ogress after a terrible battle.

It is this latter part of the story which makes it seem that the two man-eaters might have been something more than the usual Ogres. For one thing, the waters of the marsh hiss and boil from the corrosive heat of their presence, a thing much more characteristic of Dragons or of Goblins than of Ogres, who also do not usually live in water. And the domestic arrangements and the magical spells which occur in this part of the story are most un-Ogrelike. It is as if a pair of Ogres had moved into the abandoned quarters of a Water Dragon.

There is one other fact which seems to identify Beowulf's opponents as Ogres, however. It appears that the name Grendel comes from two Old Norse words meaning "storm" and "to bellow." In that case,

14

Grendel would be a very suitable name for a Teutonic Ogre, so closely related to the loud-voiced, storm-brewing Frost Giants.

A third branch of the Giant family, which has great importance in Scandinavian mythology, is that of the Trolls. Though certainly cousins of the Giants and Ogres, Trolls are in some ways different from either. For one thing, Trolls vary greatly in size. While the biggest Troll may be as large as a mountain some are hardly above human size and can live comfortably under bridges or in barns.

The major characteristic of Trolls, however, is that they seem to become a part of the land in which they live. There are Forest Trolls, Mountain Trolls, River Trolls, and though they can and do threaten human beings, it sometimes seems they are mainly guardians of their rugged and beautiful countryside.

Mountain Trolls are naturally the biggest of the family. They are reputed to have the strength of fifty men, but you are not very likely to see one (even if you believe in Trolls) because not only do they haunt the remotest and highest mountains, but they hate the sight and scent of human beings and never come out of their caves in the daytime.

That the Trolls were once part of the pagan beliefs that flourished before Christianity is indicated by the fact that they are afraid of the sound of church bells. One might say that they have been driven underground until they cannot bear the light of the sun. Some say a Troll will burst if he is caught out in the daylight, others claim he will turn to stone.

In either case the sight of a Mountain Troll coming out at sunset through the hinged stone door of his lair would be almost more awe-inspiring than frightening. Mountain Trolls are as tough and craggy as

15

their homes. Their skin is moss-covered, while shrubs grow on their ears and noses, pines on their backs. In every part they are gnarled and weathered as if with great age. They have the tails of pigs, horses, or cows, and the one with the most knots in his tail is the highest in rank. When thunder rolls it is, as one might expect, the Mountain Trolls calling to each other.

Forest Trolls are a little less formidable, but no less interesting. They often look like trees or huge, shaggy bears, and they are definitely unfriendly to woodcutters. However, they aren't any smarter than Giants or Ogres, and there is a Norwegian tale about a young man who talked a Troll into clearing a large patch of forest for him. Apparently the Troll was not the kind who turn to stone in the daylight, for he came along while this young fellow was working and began boasting of his strength. The woodsman then pointed to a large wheel of cheese which he had brought for lunch. "Do you see that stone?" he asked, and the Troll nodded. "Then watch this." The young man picked up the cheese in one hand and squeezed the whey from it. Amazed at the strength of one who could press water from a stone the Troll was forced to agree to do the job of land-clearing and of course finished the work in a fraction of the normal time.

River Trolls like those in the nursery tale of the Three Billy Goats Gruff, live near fresh water and demand a toll or forfeit from those who cross bridges in their territory.

Though they often live alone, some Trolls have a family life in their underground halls. These deep caverns shine with gold and precious gems, but that is about as far as civilization goes among the Trolls. Troll-brats are very ill-behaved and give their mothers a great deal of

Big People

17

trouble. As for the Troll-wives themselves, they spend most of their time cooking up huge meals of pig snouts, bear paws, and the like. Their cooking is not very refined, and they stir their pots with their long red noses. Sometimes the Troll-wives become so fed up with the bad behavior of their own young ones that they will steal a human baby to raise. That habit probably shows the influence of the Faery Folk.

A few Trolls are partly domesticated and have become House Trolls. That is, they have taken some isolated farm under their protection, although their usual attitude to men ranges from bare tolerance to hostility. Their ideals and values are older, wilder, and altogether different from those of men. It is said that once a boy stole a Troll's eye and when he looked through it he found that everything was reversed. Crude was fine, ugly was beautiful, bad was good. There couldn't be a better description of the outlook of the Big People in general. They are simply not human, and it is far better to leave them alone.

We have seen the way Giants and their kin appear in folklore and myth. The question still remains: Did they ever really exist, and if not, why did so many people believe in them? For there is no doubt that even in parts of the world where few would admit to such beliefs today, the time when nearly everyone believed in Giants is only four or five hundred years past. In those days people might not have expected to have their washing dried for them by the Grabbist Giant, but they were quite sure that Giants were real, that they lived in some far place or had lived in the neighborhood until just recently. Was there any truth in these ideas?

As with most complex questions, the answer to this one is Yes,

No, and Maybe. If by the word "giant" you mean a man who is much taller than average, then "giants" did exist then and still exist today. There are, for example, whole groups of people like the Watusi of central equatorial Africa among whom seven feet is by no means an unusual height. *73-266*

Another kind of genuine giant is the individual who simply grows much taller than his family and neighbors. The very tallest of such giants probably reach their immense heights because they have a physical condition in which the pituitary gland (the gland controlling the growth of the bones) becomes overactive. One of the largest giants on record was a Russian named Machnow, who appeared with an exhibition in Paris in 1905 and claimed to measure nine feet, three and a half inches tall. That is no mean size, even for a Giant in a hero-tale. It is, in fact, just about the height of Goliath, the oversize Philistine whom David slew with his slingshot according to the Bible (I Samuel, 17). The measurement given there for Goliath is six cubits and a span, but we can't know exactly how tall that was because a cubit varied from seventeen to twenty inches, while a span was about nine inches. That would put Goliath between nine feet, three inches (Machnow's height) and ten feet, nine inches. When we consider that Goliath's armor weighed eighty pounds and his spearhead alone weighed ten pounds (the measures are again approximate), we begin to appreciate David's courage. There are, then, real giants whose size would do credit to some of the Giants of legend. However, if we look at some of the more truly gigantic Giants, things are different. No being of a mere ten feet could lift up a fishing vessel and her crew like the Grabbist Giant, or carry off the bodies of thirty men like Grendel.

There are many places in the world which were formerly pointed to as evidence for the existence of Giants whose height was measured in **hundreds**, rather than in tens of feet. In sandstone, limestone, coal, and other fossil-bearing rocks, one can occasionally see what are obviously huge bones. Today we know that the largest of those bones belonged to the dinosaurs, the great reptiles that became extinct long before man made his appearance on earth. In centuries past, however, such enormous remains were thought to be those of Giants or Dragons.

Sometimes features of the landscape were said to have been constructed by Giants. The best known of these is probably the Giants' Causeway, a line of huge and strangely even stones which extends into the sea from a promontory in northern Ireland. Other places in the British Isles which were attributed to Giants' work are Wansdyke, Wenlock Edge, and Maes Knoll. The rocks called Steep Holme and Flat Holme in the Bristol Channel were said to be Giants' bones.

Scientists say that one good reason there never were human-shaped creatures big enough to raise mountains or dig out valleys such as these is that a man of that size would be so heavy he would break his own bones. The gravity of Earth is too strong to let its animals grow that tall.

But it is rather hard to say goodbye to the Giants just yet, for in all our researches we have not found explanations for some of their most universal characteristics. We would still like to know why the Giants and their kin live in caves under the mountains, why they are so slow mentally, why they seem to have no arts or civilization, and above all, why most of them eat human flesh. Perhaps we should look for the answers, not in folklore, but in the sciences of anthropology, archeology, and paleontology—the studies of *Homo sapiens*, his ancient civilizations, and fossil remains. For if you were to describe a creature who looks like an Ogre and has the habits just listed, an anthropologist might well say, "Of course. That's *pithecanthropus*." He would be referring to one of the early types of prehistoric man, whose fossil bones show that he did not belong to our species, *Homo sapiens*. The remains of *pithecanthropus* have been found as far apart as China, Java, Kenya, Algeria, and Germany. Looking at reconstructions of his probable appearance, it is hard to resist the conclusion that *pithecanthropus* would have made a perfect Ogre. His portraits usually show him with heavy brows, backward-sloping forehead, large forward-thrusting jaws, long arms, and stooping shoulders. The skeletons do not tell us whether *pithecanthropus* was a great deal hairier than modern man, but many scientists think that he was. We also know that at least one type of *pithecanthropus* was a cannibal. His remains have been found together with a number of smashed skulls that showed that the brains had been scooped out as if from a bowl of porridge. Another type of the species is thought to have been between eight and ten feet in height, a measurement based on the great size and weight of his skull. It is only necessary to add that many of these skeletons have been discovered in caves and to remark that *pithecanthropus* is believed to have been replaced by more advanced species of man because of their superior intelligence. The picture is almost perfect.

In fact, the picture is too perfect. Before we can identify the original cannibal Giant with *pithecanthropus* or any other type of prehistoric man, we will have to get over two Giant-size difficulties. The first is that it is entirely possible that no man as we know him ever saw a living *pithecanthropus*. As far as can be discovered from fossils, *Homo sapiens* did not appear on earth until about 75,000 years ago, while the latest *pithecanthropus* is at least one million years dead. Now although a difference of 925,000 years is not a very long one in terms of evolution, there is *no* positive evidence to show that *pithecanthropus* survived into the period of our earliest direct ancestors.

But even if *pithecanthropus* the Ogre did live to make a few meals off his smaller and brainier cousins, there is doubt that the tales and legends that have come down to us could be anything like as accurate as they seem to be. After all, every bit of human history as we define history has taken place in the last 6,000 years, which leaves something like 70,000 years unaccounted for by written records. The once popular idea that human beings have a sort of racial memory of past conditions, as hereditary as hair color, is no longer thought to be sound. Thus we would have to believe either that the experience of meeting real-life Giants or Ogres had been passed down through thousands of generations by word of mouth alone or that whichever form of early man inspired the legends survived much longer than he is usually given credit for.

The best we can do at this time is keep an open mind about the whole matter. We may never know whether it is just coincidence that so many stories of the Big People sound like those of a less developed human species—one that lives in caves because it has not learned to build, that has not mastered the sword or even the bow and arrow, that plants no crops, follows no trades, and, like certain very primitive human tribes—and Ogres—has no words for the numerals beyond five.

In discussing the subject of Giants, there is one more being we ought to consider. Since 1899 the remote heights of the Himalaya mountains have been the source of strange rumors concerning a creature called the yeti. There, it has sometimes seemed, was a live myth that might turn into fact. The yeti is better known as the Abominable Snowman, but that name is misleading since the creature, real or imaginary, may be dangerous but hardly seems abominable and probably doesn't spend most of its time in the snow.

The first report of the yeti to reach the world at large seems to have been a book by Major L. A. Waddell, in which he told of finding a trail of unusual and outsize footprints in northeastern Sikkim in 1899. Waddell had been told by the people of the region that the prints belonged to "one of the large hairy wild men who are believed to live amongst the eternal snows." Since that time expeditions into that little-known area have confirmed that the yeti is believed in—under different names—over an area of thousands of square miles which includes parts of Tibet, Nepal, Sikkim, Bhutan, Assam, and northern Burma. The reports of the mountain people agree on the yeti's general description. It is a huge creature halfway between man and beast. Its face is light colored and rather human looking, while the rest of its body is dark and shaggy with thick, bowed legs, inward turning toes, and arms that reach down to its knees like those of the gorilla and other apes. It lives in caves on the highest and wildest slopes of those highest and wildest mountains in the world, and it is enormously strong. Like a true Giant the yeti is said to be able to uproot sizable trees and to lift great boulders. Some reports say it will attack and even eat men; others describe it as shy and harmless except when provoked.

For years the tales of the yeti were thought to be mere superstition on the part of the mountain people, and so they may be—simply another version of the universal Giant story. However, those who say they know the yeti are quick to state that it is not a "spirit being" but a real one, showing that the difference is perfectly plain in their minds. We might also remark that western Europeans have a long record of disbelief in "native tales." White men always seem to think they know more about a place than do the people who have lived there for centuries. Perfectly real animals whose existence has been pooh-poohed in this way include the mountain gorilla, the frozen mammoths of Siberia, the giant monitor lizard called the Komodo dragon, and the Asian tapir.

Furthermore, traces of the yeti and what is supposed to be the creature itself have in recent decades been seen by increasing numbers of westerners, ranging from the renowned mountain climber, Eric Shipton, to scientists Gerald Russell and Charles Stonor—and even Prince Peter of Greece. Anyone who wishes can now collect dozens of accounts by persons who certainly saw *something* in the area in question. However, there is not nearly enough space here to give the whole history of the yeti in detail.* The subject is a very complex one, partly because most of the evidence of the yeti's existence is in the form of footprints. And, Sherlock Holmes notwithstanding, the study of footprints is a difficult business in which many conflicting interpretations are possible. That is especially true when the prints in question may be those of an unknown animal and were made in snow, which can inconveniently melt, freeze, or drift, obscuring the evidence. There is no doubt at all that some of the tracks supposedly made by the yeti can actually be attributed to bears, snow leopards, or langurs (rather large local monkeys that sometimes go above the snow line).

*Those who wish to read further on this topic might consult Ivan T. Sanderson's fascinating book ABOMINABLE SNOWMEN (Philadelphia: Chilton Book Co., 1961).

It is also disappointing to have to note that though several claims have been made for the existence of preserved yeti scalps, the only items of this kind to be examined scientifically turned out to be in one case a crude fake and in another, a piece of skin from a Nepalese goat called the serow, stretched and molded into the conical shape that is supposed to be that of the yeti's skull. This may not mean that no such scalps exist, for the lamas (monastic Tibetan priests) who claim to possess them believe that the scalps are both very ancient and very sacred and are understandably unwilling to hand them over for study by outsiders. And we must not suppose that because some are fakes there can be no genuine scalps, just as a horse painted with black stripes doesn't prove there are no zebras. In any case, the matter has been closed to western investigators since the absorption of Tibet by the People's Republic of China, which has imposed severe limitations on visitors.

After disposing of a great deal of mistaken and misleading evidence concerning the yeti, the positive case can be summarized as follows. There are some as yet unexplained reports from apparently reliable persons who say they have seen a large hairy animal of roughly human shape walking—not moving with the use of its hands like a monkey or standing on its hind legs like a bear—in the barren snow fields above an altitude of 10,000 feet and sometimes as high as 16,000 feet. Likewise there are drawings and photographs of the tracks of this animal which seem to show that it walks for much greater distances on its hind legs than bears are ever known to do; that its stride is too long for a man's, let alone a monkey's; that it does not have an opposable thumb or great toe as do all the large apes; that it has its largest toe on the inside like a man rather than on the outside like a bear; and finally, that it is a biped

25

and not a four-footed creature which puts its hind feet directly on top of the prints of its forefeet (as some animals indeed do, thus giving its tracks the appearance of those of a biped).

Furthermore, though it comes as a surprise to most people, the yeti is not the only large man-ape creature to have been reported from remote areas. North and South America, where there are no known species of true apes, harbor strange tales from such places as the densely forested upper peninsula of Michigan and the remoter parts of California (where the beast is called the sasquatch), and the still largely unexplored jungles of the Amazon basin. Stories from the last-named region contain the interesting if gory detail that herds of cattle have been found slaughtered with no apparent injury except that their tongues have been torn out, an act that some say would be hard to accomplish except with an extraordinarily strong *hand*. In Asia similar unknown creatures have been reported as far apart as the Gobi desert and Sumatra.

What are we to make of all this vagueness? Evidence from these other parts of the world is even less solid than that for the yeti. It would certainly be exciting if we were to discover the survivors of the great man-apes or early men who are known to have roamed the earth hundreds of thousands of years ago. But wishful thinking is not enough. Is it *possible*? To that we can only say that man does not, perhaps, know as much about his world as he would like to think. The six-foot fish called the coelacanth was supposed to have been extinct for seventy *million* years until a live specimen was brought up in a fisherman's net in 1938. And it was only a year earlier that the first giant panda was captured. Perhaps there is the barest possibility (we can put it no more strongly than that) that the story of the Giants is not ended.

II
THE FAERY FOLK

Come away, O human child!
To the waters and the wild
With a faery, hand in hand,
For the world's more full of weeping
than you can understand.

—W. B. Yeats

MOST PEOPLE know exactly what Faeries are like. They are tiny little creatures with magic wands, and they are usually female. They have gauzy wings, and they flutter around flowers or ride on bumblebees.

Nonsense. Such a being would be about as much like a true Faery as a glass of pink lemonade is like the ocean. Unfortunately the Faery Folk have been distorted and misunderstood by those who never bothered to know them properly. Beginning as early as the sixteenth century, but mainly in the nineteenth, writers and artists produced so many examples of what they thought Faeries *ought to be* like that they almost entirely blotted out the image of what folktales and myths had said they *were*. During that period there was a great tendency to make things "nice" and to reduce everything to a manageable size, especially any-

27

thing that man's new sciences had not been able to explain. So the Faeries began to be thought of as cute, and little, and "nice." What a transformation.

The true Faery Folk come from Brittany, Wales, Scotland, Ireland, Devon, Cornwall, and to a lesser extent from Scandinavia and the remaining parts of northern Europe. That is to say that the Faery tradition survives mainly in those lands that have the largest populations of the Celtic people. As recently as the early years of this century there were folk in the more out-of-the-way parts of those places who still spoke of the Good People, as the Faeries were sometimes called, as if they were neighbors. And if the Faeries were seldom actually seen, the signs of their existence were supposed to be all around. The Faery Folk travel under many names, and the tales that are told of them vary from place to place, but one can gather a great deal about them by reading the hundreds of tales in which they appear.

Tall they are, and beautiful beyond mere mortal beauty. Theirs are slenderness and grace and lightness of foot, and they love all quick-moving things and music and dancing. Their halls lie under lakes or beneath stones or inside the hollow hills, those ancient knolls that often turn out to contain prehistoric burial sites. Like human beings in centuries past, the Faeries are ruled by a king. They also make love or war and ride to the hunt but there the likeness ends. The storytellers know them to be far older than man, both as a race and as individuals. No one knows their life span, but it is several times as long as a man's, and though it is true that they do cease to exist in the end, Faeries never grow old. They are great masters of magic and all ancient knowledge, with which they can do wonders that no human being can comprehend.

Faery time is quite different from our time. It does not appear to flow at an even rate, but may go either faster or slower. Thus in an old tale a man who visits the Faeries in their own land returns to discover that decades have passed in what had seemed only an hour. Equally well, the visitor may return an old man filled with a lifetime of experiences, only to find his friends not an hour older than he left them.

Faeries are as unpredictable as their time. They value valiant deeds and honor and truthfulness, but they can be dangerous because human standards of right and wrong are alien to them. They are not evil any more than fire is evil (though you may be burned if you interfere with it).

Faeries can be generous and even helpful, but they are very quick to take offense. Three things one must never do are to injure a Faery tree, to approach a Faery with iron, or to name the Faeries out loud. The last is especially hazardous, for names are very powerful magic everywhere. It is much better to speak of the Faeries as the Good Folk, the People of Peace, the Fair Folk, the Seely (Holy) Court, the Good Neighbors, or any of a host of other names by which they have gone. In Ireland they are called the Sidhe, pronounced "Shee." As for the name Faery itself, it comes from the Latin word *Fata*, meaning Fate or a being with magical powers, which gives an indication of why it is advisable to show the Faeries you think well of them by calling them something flattering. The other, more important reason for the practice is that in some places if you mention a Faery by name it is as if you were summoning him. Once you have done that he has power over you and can take you away forever.

One of the best tales of the way Faeries deal with mortals comes

30

from Cornwall. A little girl was out picking primroses one day and wandered into the rocky place called Goblin Combe. In her playing she happened to knock on a stone, which surprised her by opening into a door in the hillside. Out of the door came the Faery Folk, who played with the child all day and then sent her home safely with the gift of a beautiful golden ball.

Now there was a conjurer in the town who heard of the little girl's adventure and thought he would try his luck at getting such a nice bit of gold. So he gathered up some primroses and went knocking on the stone. But says the tale, " 'twasn't the right day, nor the right number of primroses, and he wasn't no dear little girl, *so they took him!*"

No one has been able to say for sure what is real in the Faery world and what is not. They cast spells on human senses so that what is rough and coarse may seem fine and beautiful. This sort of illusion is called glamour, and it takes a determined man to resist it.

Such a one, apparently, was the early Christian Saint Collen, who is reported to have visited a Faery palace that had the habit of appearing on top of England's Glastonbury Tor. He found there a great hall bright with torches and filled with music, feasting, and laughter, where Faery lords and ladies were served by pages dressed in red and blue. The diners offered him food and drink, which Saint Collen wisely refused to accept, for if he had, he might have been forced to remain with his hosts forever. Instead, he sprinkled the gathering with holy water, whereupon lights were doused, music died, and the revellers disappeared. Except that the hero of the tale was a Saint, this is a typical account of a Faery feast.

The Faeries are rich in beautiful things, as notable for their work-

manship as for their value. Gold and silver are theirs in plenty, as well as fine harps, drinking cups, finger rings, and horses. They also possess cloaks that can make the wearer invisible. The Faeries' usual costume is green or white, although they also like red, and their favorite food is reported to be milk and saffron. One thing never found among the Faeries, however, is an object made of iron. They hate iron which may be the origin of the tradition that it is lucky to hang a horseshoe over your door. No house so protected will ever be bothered by Faery mischief.

There is no doubt that the Faery Folk sometimes bring trouble to human beings. One of their most usual habits was to steal a human child, leaving their own young one in the baby's place. The child thus substituted was called a changeling and could be told by its shriveled, unhealthy appearance. Quite often the human mother would raise the changeling as her own, either because the exchange had not been detected or out of pity for the strange child's helplessness. In areas where belief in Faeries was strong any child who did not resemble the rest of its family stood a good chance of being taken for a changeling and was sometimes shunned for that reason. The situation must have been hard on some perfectly ordinary children whose heredity made them tall in a short family or dark-haired in a blond one.

The tales say that in some cases the parents were not willing to accept the changeling. There were then two things they could do. The first was to trick the Faery child into revealing its true nature. For that the recommended method was to brew ale in an eggshell while the infant watched. Changelings are unlike human children in that they can talk and reason as soon as they are born, and Faery lives are so much longer than ours that a seeming infant may be older than its human "mother."

Thus since ale is of course usually brewed in large casks or kegs, the sight of someone brewing in an eggshell was very astonishing to the changeling. In one story the infant gave itself away by exclaiming, "I am old, old, ever so old. I have seen three forests grow and wither, but I never saw ale brewed in an eggshell before." Once the masquerade is ended in this way, the changeling's true parents can be forced to take it back and restore the human child.

The second way of dealing with changelings is more dangerous. The stolen child's father must go to the nearest Faery hill on a moonlit night, when the Faery palace will be visible, rising out of the ground on pillars. The man must take with him a dagger, a Bible, and a rooster. Plunging the iron weapon into the side of the hill will break the enchantments so he can enter and find his child. The Bible will protect him while he is inside. As for the rooster, its daybreak crowing has always made it a symbol of the triumph of daylight over the dangers of darkness, and the sound is effective against evil temptations.

In that connection, it is interesting to note that the Faery Folk are said to keep all the usual domestic animals except cats and chickens. Probably this is because the cat and the domestic fowls were not introduced into Britain until after the Faery legends had become well established. Otherwise, the tales give the impression that the Faeries are excellent livestock breeders. Their cattle are sleek and fat, usually white or red in color. One may often see Faery herds grazing, but they will disappear into the hillside if approached too closely. Faery hunting hounds are the finest and some Faery gathering places are protected by great black dogs with eyes the size of saucers. As for the horses of Faeryland, they are like their masters—almost too swift and spirited to be flesh and blood.

The Faery Folk

Among the creatures of the everyday world the Faeries have under their special protection cattle, horses, goats, pigs, birds, salmon, trout, and deer. Their favorite trees are the oak and the elder, but all trees and wild things are in their keeping.

As we have seen from the example of the changelings, the stories show that the Faery Folk are not completely independent of the human world, much as they like to stay aloof from human affairs. In fact, there are several other points at which the two worlds may touch. For one thing, Faeries often marry mortals. Both men and women have been stolen away to live within the hollow hills, especially if they are beautiful and love music. In Ireland the Ganconer, or "Love Talker," is supposed to be a handsome Faery youth who wins the hearts of mortal girls with his sweet words. If they refuse to go with him into that other land where time has no meaning, they will pine away and die. An old song from the Hebrides is said to be the spell of a Faery lover:

Why should I sit and sigh
(Pool and bracken, pool and bracken)
Why should I sit and sigh
On the hillside dreary?

When I see the plover rising
Or the curlew wheeling,
Then I trow my mortal lover
Back to me is stealing.

When the day wears away,
Sad I look a-down the valley:
Ilka sound wae a stound
Sets my heart a thrillin'.

Ah, but there is something wanting
Oh, but I am weary.
Come, my blithe and bonnie lass,
Come o'er the knowe to cheer me.

Perhaps it is to care for these stolen brides that the Faeries are occasionally forced to kidnap human midwives. At any rate, there are many tales of a village midwife summoned in the middle of the night, not to a house, but to a Faery hall under hill or lake. Sometimes the old woman safely delivers the baby and is conducted home with a fine gift of gold, only to find she cannot remember how to find the entrance to the Faery realm. In another version of the story the midwife was given an ointment to rub on the newborn child and accidentally got some of the ointment into one of her own eyes. The next day she was surprised to meet the Faery lord who had summoned her. When she greeted him he asked which eye she saw him with and on being told, quickly put out the eye with his dagger. That may seem a harsh punishment for learning Faery secrets, but the Faeries have long ago learned to be ruthless in protecting themselves from human intervention.

Many of the tales say that one of the best chances for a mortal to observe the Faeries is to come upon one of their markets—that is, if he is willing to pay the price. In parts of the British Isles one may sometimes see upon the open moor a fine fair with stalls of goods or produce for sale and many figures in high-crowned hats. Once a curious farmer came upon such a market on Blackdowne Heath and decided to go in among the stalls and sample the Faery wares. He could see the market clearly as he rode toward it, but as soon as he came to the spot itself everything disappeared. Yet the man knew he had not merely imagined what he saw because he felt himself pushed and jostled unmercifully as if by an invisible crowd. And it is said that after his experience the farmer was not only black and blue but lame for life as a reminder that one should not try to meddle in Faery business.

No one has truly seen the Faeries, however, unless he has watched them dance as some have claimed to have done. On moon-bright nights, and especially on May Eve or Midsummer Eve, the Faery Folk come to their ancient gathering places, the prehistoric stone circles, hill forts, long barrows, and standing stones that dot the countryside even today. There they join hands in the Faery Ring and dance the night away to the music of harps and voices. Those who have been fortunate enough to come upon the scene say that there is such silvery fire in the shifting forms of the dance as to make a mere mortal weep for his own heavy feet and awkward moving.

"Faeries dancing under the moon,/ A Druid land, a Druid tune." That is the way the Faery Ring was described by the great Irish poet William Butler Yeats, who is also quoted at the opening of this chapter. Yeats was much interested in his country's folklore, especially that concerning the Faeries and, now that we have met the true Faeries, Yeats' lines bring us back to the question we asked earlier about the Giants: Who were they?

One of the many names under which the Faeries were known provides us with an important clue to Faery origins. In Ireland they are often called the Tuatha De Danann, "People of the Goddess Danu," and ancient Irish manuscripts reveal that this was also the name by which the pre-Christian Celts referred to their gods. If, like the Giants, the Faeries had their origins in mythology, it is no wonder that they have carried down to us some of the power and beauty of the gods they once were. The theory is supported by the fact that the names of some of the Faery Folk in the earliest tales are the same as those of the Celtic gods. Even now we say that an idea or thing is part of "the underground" when it is kept secret because it has been condemned by the authorities. Perhaps it is in that sense that the Faeries went underground to live when the old beliefs fell out of favor. We have already seen that for pagan deities to be downgraded in this way is not at all uncommon, and we shall find still more examples of the process in later chapters. However, it is not enough to say that the Faeries were *only* folk memories of the Celtic gods. The tales about them are too specific and full of details that have nothing to do with what we know of Celtic mythology.

To follow the Faeries further we shall have to consider a few facts about prehistoric Britain. The British Isles were separated from the European mainland by water sometime during the Ice Ages and their subsequent history is that of a series of invasions from the continent. It was in that way that the Celts arrived. They were an Iron Age people who had crossed Europe in a few centuries of migration from western Germany and eastern France. The Celts probably did not arrive in Britain much earlier than the sixth century B.C., a relatively late period in British history, when the great feat of construction engineering that is Stonehenge was already a thousand years old.

This is the point at which the story becomes unbearably complicated. In spite of the burial sites, stone circles, and other remains they left behind them, we know very little about the people who inhabited Britain before the Celts arrived. Almost the only thing of which we can

38

be sure is that the men who could shape the huge stones of Stonehenge without the aid of iron tools, transport them without wheels over two hundred forty miles from where they had been quarried in Wales, and place them so accurately that they could be used as an astronomical observatory for predicting eclipses and for marking the motions of the sun and moon, cannot have been the semi-bestial savages that some history books have made them out to be.

Those pre-Celtic peoples, who probably did not themselves all belong to the same tribe and level of culture, were conquered and largely erased by the Celts, and if Britain's history had stopped there we might know a great deal more about the answer to the problem of the Faery Folk. Instead, the islands were subjected to further waves of invasion, first by the Romans and later (and more permanently) by the Angles, Jutes, Saxons, Danes, and other Teutonic tribes, and finally by the Normans. For nearly a thousand years the land was fought over, raided, parcelled out by treaty, and reconquered. At the end of that period the Celts themselves were in much the same position as their predecessors. They had been pushed entirely out of the rich central portion of England into the wild mountains of Wales and Scotland, into the remote southern peninsula now occupied by Devon and Cornwall, and into Ireland. The bitterness felt by the Celts toward their conquerors (who later came to be called English) has lingered even into the present.

This brings us back to the Tuatha De Danann, the Faeries, and Yeats' verse, which mentions the Druids. Since the last century there have been many who noticed how much the behavior of the Faery Folk sounds like that of a conquered people—their secrecy, exclusiveness, underground dwellings, and so forth. Yeats and others assumed that the Faeries were, in a sense, the conquered Celts themselves, their gods gone underground. The Druids (priests of the Celtic religion) were seen as belonging to a cult whose celebrations included the ritual dance of the Faery Ring at sacred spots such as Stonehenge. Now, however, it is known that the Druids and their people were not the builders of Stonehenge, and there is not even much indication that they used it after the earlier folk had been driven out. Beyond that is the fact that the earliest Irish documents clearly state that the Tuatha (before they became gods) were a separate people living in Ireland prior to the arrival of those who made the records, a branch of the Celts calling themselves Milesians. Possibly the Druids do not really belong to Yeats' poem because though they were also forced "underground" by the advent of Christianity and many memories of pagan Celtic life are found in the tales of the Sidhe Folk, the Druids were not the inspiration for the original Faeries. That place must be given to some of the pre-Celtic peoples of whom we know so little.

Now let us look in more detail at these beings who haunt the modern Celtic imagination. If we are wondering whether they were Celts or pre-Celts there is one very striking fact to consider—their hatred and fear of iron. The Celts, as has been said before, were an Iron Age people, but the pre-Celts plainly were not. In fact, it was probably the Celts' superior iron weapons which in part enabled them to conquer the earlier inhabitants, *who knew only stone and bronze.* In the Orkney and Shetland islands the flint arrowheads which often turn up in the soil are called elf shot or Faery arrows, to this day. Surely a people whose weapons were made of flint and soft bronze would have feared and hated the iron that made their enemies invincible, perhaps in the same way that the native Americans were overawed by the guns of the first Europeans.

Consider, too, how much the Faeries sound like fugitives, a people

41

in hiding from their conquerors, rather than an underground religious movement. They are hard to find, often invisible, which may simply mean that in their green clothing they are masters of the art of concealment. In some areas they are called the Silent Moving Ones. Like any group engaged in guerrilla warfare, they come by stealth and never fight a pitched battle. There are many stories of travelers led astray by strange moving lights on moors or marshes, sometimes to their deaths. Those who eventually returned home often told of the sound of mocking laughter that followed them as they stumbled through the dark, though the laughers themselves were not to be seen. Perhaps the Will O' the Wisp was not always the blue flame of ignited marsh gas, as has been claimed.

A proud people on the brink of starvation might also act in a way that is often reported of Faeries, though of a less noble and heroic kind than the great lords and ladies who have had most of our attention in this chapter. For there is a very odd disagreement in Faery legends, some of which deal with the tall and beautiful Tuatha De Danann and others with folk of human size or a little smaller. In the stories, though both are called Faeries, it is the little dark ones who steal from the careless housewife. They also do farm work or household chores for those who will leave them a bowl of milk, a bag of salt, a cooking pot, or other useful items. It is as if those who are too proud to steal will still do work in order to keep from starving.*

Finally, there is the matter of the changelings. All kinds of theories have been proposed concerning this peculiar tradition. Some say it is an

*These small Faeries who do both useful work and mischief are more correctly called Brownies or Pixies and will be discussed fully in Chapter III. However, their Faery ancestry is indisputable.

explanation for the sudden illnesses of formerly healthy infants or that it has to do with the doctrine of transmigration of souls. But somewhere in the back of the mind there lingers an image of a desperate people, driven out of prosperous farmlands and valleys to scrape a living from the rocky hills. In bad seasons, perhaps, when they saw their own children grow weak and withered from lack of food, they might have stolen down to the rich farms and left their little ones in the place of the fat, healthy babies of the conquerors—a double revenge for years of oppression. It is an intriguing picture, and as with so many other "explanations" of legend, it is too bad we can't be more certain about it. There are those who argue that the Faeries never had anything to do with real people, pre-Celtic or otherwise, but were merely the souls of the dead— who were invisible, who stole away the young and beautiful, and who came out of the ground like ghosts the world over. As with so much of what is in this book: we do not know.

Before leaving the Faery Folk, however, there are one or two other branches of the family which, though not part of the central Celtic tradition, certainly belong under the same heading. One may have wondered, for example, why in all this discussion there has been no mention of Faery Godmothers. The reason is that those ladies with magic wands are part of the Faery lore of France and have little to do with the Tuatha De Danann. That Faery Godmothers are a relatively late development is easily seen from the fact that they are godmothers at all, since a Christian ceremony is the last place where one would look for a being out of the pagan past. In fact, Faery Godmothers were hardly heard of in England until the seventeenth century, when they were introduced to a wide audience through the publication of Perrault's collection of so-called fairy tales—"so-called fairy tales" because it must be clear by now that the French stories and the later collection of the Grimm brothers hardly deal with real Faeries at all. There are plenty of Giants in them, to be sure, as well as Witches, Ogres, Sorcerers, Dragons, and an occasional Dwarf, Brownie, or Goblin, but aside from the ladies with magical powers who make gifts to newborn children there isn't a genuine Faery to be seen. We must conclude that (with the exception of Brittany, which has a large Celtic population and strong Faery traditions) the Faeries in France were quite thoroughly neglected in later centuries and reduced to the status of mere court hangers-on.

Even farther from the land of the Tuatha De Danann is Scandinavia. Yet there we find tales of the Hulderfolk, or "Hidden People," who sound exactly like true Faeries in almost every way. The only striking difference is that the Hulderfolk had tails, rather as if there were a Troll or so in their ancestry. Yet they were not Trolls, for not only were they not Troll size, but they were beautiful, lived in underground palaces, and liked to marry mortals. The tales say that if a young man could persuade a Hulder-maiden to be married to him in church, she would lose her tail and become in all ways like a human wife. Such marriages were very lucky, for the Hulderfolk always saw to it that the couple prospered. Their children, while normal in other ways, were blessed with the power of reading the past and future, called second sight, and could also understand the speech of animals. The descendants of the Hulderfolk are the ones, in Norwegian tradition, who become the great storytellers, because of their special gift of words and poetic vision. These talents are also associated with the Faeries in Scotland,

Ireland, and Wales. One might wish for a bit of second sight in solving some of the riddles posed by the Faery Folk in this chapter, for the Hidden People themselves will not tell us the answers.

Like so many of the finest creations of human imagination, the Faeries are leaving us, dying out when belief fails and they are exiled to the realm of mere superstition. In this case, however, the tales themselves recognize what is happening. They say that the Faery Folk have one final refuge, toward which they will shortly set sail, if they have not already done so. Far across the western sea lies Tir na nOg, "The Land of the Ever Young." As long ago as the seventeenth century, storytellers told of meeting cavalcades of Faeries riding down to the sea. The human world had become too crowded, too selfish and unfeeling for them, the riders said. Soon they would leave entirely. And there are some who say the world will be a grayer and duller place without them.

III
LITTLE PEOPLE

Up the airy mountain,
Down the rushy glen,
We daren't go a-hunting,
For fear of little men.

—William Allingham

THERE NEVER WAS a farm or household so well run that minor things didn't seem to happen without explanation. A fallen cake, a missing tool, a strayed cow back in the barn, a sudden noise in an apparently empty room, a dropped plate that didn't break—sometimes it certainly seems as if there must be little beings whose purpose is to make (or occasionally prevent) trouble for humanity and many tales are told of them. They are house spirits, and though they go by different names, stories about them must be as old as the human habit of building houses.

The best-known house guardian of this kind is the Brownie. All over the north of England and also in Cornwall and Scotland, the Brownie is regarded as a very lucky creature to have about the house, for his bits of mischief are greatly outweighed by the useful work he does at night after the family has gone to bed. Brownies are very good at churning butter, spinning thread, carding wool, and generally straightening things up. Apparently they like to keep busy, too, for they will sometimes make a thorough mess of a house that has been left so neat there is nothing for them to do.

The Brownie is quite touchy about his work and usually prefers to be left alone, though he will accept a dish of bread and milk in a quiet corner. The best way to frighten him off is to try to sneak up on him or catch him, and the next best way is to pay him for his work. A Brownie is absolutely certain to vanish if you give him a suit of clothes.

The Brownie is friendly with all domestic animals, especially cats, cows, and goats, and he is exceptionally good at handling bees. In Cornwall when the bees swarm, one should go outside and beat on a tin pan while shouting, "Brownie! Brownie!" Then the Brownie will take charge of the swarm and make sure the bees find a good home in the neighborhood.

In appearance, the Brownie is usually brown (not very surprisingly). He has a sharp, pointed nose and sometimes pointed ears. No one is sure exactly how tall a Brownie is, but a good guess would be about two feet.

Some individual Brownies have become famous in legend. There was, for example, the Brownie Hob of Yorkshire who lived in a cave called the Hobhole. Parents of children with whooping cough used to bring them to the hole's entrance and call out, "Hobhole Hob! Hobhole Hob! My bairn's got kincough. Tak't off! Tak't off!" The children were always supposed to recover—maybe because they were so anxious to catch a glimpse of Hobhole Hob.

49

In the English border country lived the Dobie, a rather clownish Brownie who was called on to guard hidden treasure. Unlike Hob, however, he was not very good at his job, for thieves often outwitted the Dobie and stole the treasure.

The illustrious Rumpelstiltskin may or may not have been a true Brownie, though he was certainly some sort of relative. You will remember that he could spin straw into gold, a very Brownie-ish trait, and that the Queen in the story was required to guess his name. In the English version of the old German tale, however, the name of the creature is Tom Tit Tot, and he is described as a black thing with a long tail, making him more of an Imp than a Brownie.

In both stories the Queen was lucky that she was protected by knowing the Brownie's name, for in other cases when Brownies are seriously annoyed they can turn into Boggarts or Bogles and devote themselves entirely to mischief and unkind pranks. The activities of the Boggart sound exactly like those of an occurrence called the poltergeist phenomenon, in which dishes, fire irons, and other objects are seen to hurl themselves about the house without the help of human hands. This noisy, destructive, and sometimes dangerous happening has been observed in many otherwise perfectly ordinary households and neither scientists nor those who believe in occultism have offered an entirely satisfactory explanation for it. Whether one calls it a poltergeist or a Boggart, it is something to avoid.

In contrast to the Brownies, who usually appear one at a time, are the Pixies, who go about in troupes. The Pixies are in all ways more closely related to the true Faeries of the last chapter than are the

50

Brownies. In fact, their name may be derived from that of the Picts, a group of ancient, and probably pre-Celtic, inhabitants of Britain. However, the Pixies have become so unlike the tall Faery Folk in looks and habits that they can hardly be called the same beings, and though some have said that the Pixies may be seen riding about the countryside like the Faeries, their mounts are not spirited horses but shaggy ponies no bigger than dogs. Some accounts say that Pixies look just like small people, but in others they have squinny eyes and hairy bodies. They are especially common in Devon and Cornwall, where they will help out with farm work and household chores. Like the Brownies and Faeries, their preferred reward for this work is a bowl of bread and milk. They also have the Faery habit of stealing children and some say they use a magic ointment to keep the child from growing.

Pixies are among the worst offenders at the game of leading travelers away from the path and into desolate places, but that is their only serious mischief. This habit of theirs was once so widely known in Cornwall that a common expression for losing one's way is to be "Pixie-led."

Some interesting stories from the same region claim that the Pixies and other Little People became shrunk, as it were, from their original Faery size. One tale has it that the Faeries' magic allows them to change shape, but that each form they take on must be smaller than the last. Another version says the Pixies are constantly getting smaller because they are (and this is an intriguing detail) the *souls* of the country's ancient inhabitants, which fade away as their memory dies out.

Cornwall once had still another kind of little folk, who were known as the Muryans. They looked and acted very much like the Pixies, except that the stories assure us they were *not* Pixies but had once been

51

beings of more than human size (that is, Faeries) who for some crime were condemned to dwindle year by year until at last they became the size of ants and then disappeared entirely.

In Brittany the mischievous but helpful household spirits are called Lutins, while the more Faerylike little Corrigans live under ancient stone monuments, dance in circles, mislead travelers, and so forth. It is curious that the Corrigans are said not to be able to go beyond Friday in naming the days of the week, perhaps because Saturday and Sunday are holy days.

The Little People of Ireland are among the best known in the world, though they are often miscalled Leprechauns. To do so is incorrect since in the Irish language "leprechaun" means simply a Faery shoemaker. To meet a whole tribe of Leprechauns would be as unlikely as to encounter a whole busload of shoemakers.

Though small, the Irish Little People have remained closer to their Faery ancestors than have most of their relatives in the rest of the British Isles. They still dress in green and red, dance in rings, and remember much of the old magic. Like the Irish themselves, the Little People are famous talkers. No matter how wily you are about catching one of them in order to make him lead you to hidden treasure, he is almost certain to talk you or trick you out of it in the end.

Another sort of small being found in the British Isles is the Hob, or Hobgoblin, not to be confused with the Brownie of Hobhole. The Hob is a kindly hearth spirit who lives in kitchens and watches over such things as the raising of bread. He has even been known to keep harm from babies when their mothers are out. The Hob is much less human-looking than the Brownie. He is not only small, but wizened, shaggy, and ragged. He may have no toes or fingers and almost no nose. Mothers and nannies sometimes used to frighten bad children with tales about the Hobgoblin, but that was a slur on his reputation. The Hob is harmless, in spite of his grotesque appearance.

In German-speaking lands one hears of Kobolds, who resemble both Brownies and Pixies. They are pictured as little men who seem very old, yet spry and nimble. They wear pointed hoods and do helpful tasks such as chopping wood, feeding the cattle, drawing water. They are also very thievish, however, and will make off with whatever they can carry.

Generally, Kobolds spend more time in the farmyard than in the house, and they make their homes in stables, barns, and cellars. It is lucky to have them around—who wouldn't be happy to have all that work done?—but they will take revenge on anyone who forgets their payment of milk and scraps from the table. As with the changeling child, one can get power over them by brewing ale in an eggshell. They have some very close relatives called *Heinzelmännchen*, who wear tall red hats.

The Slavic peoples of Russia and central Europe tell tales of several kinds of small beings who lived in and around houses. The commonest of these was the Domovoi. He was usually a little man covered with silky fur, even on the palms of his hands, although sometimes he could appear as an animal or a bundle of hay. The Domovoi was seldom seen, but his moans, groans, whispers, and mutterings could be heard at all hours. It was said that he was benevolent, however, and could be relied on to alert the inhabitants of the house if trouble threatened, or to warn the wife when her husband was going to beat her. The Domovoi's favorite spot was beside the stove or under the threshold, but his wife, who was called the Domania, preferred the cellar. They often became so attached to a house that they might not want to leave it when the family moved.

If a man built a new house his wife had to be sure to put a slice of bread under the stove to attract the Domovoi and the Domania.

Outside the house lived the Dvorovoi and the Ovinnik, the first in the yard and the second in the barn. They were less well disposed than the Domovoi, but might be frightened into good behavior. The Dvorovoi and the Ovinnik both sometimes appeared as little hairy men, although the Ovinnik could also take the shape of a large, untidy black cat. He lived in a corner of the barn and could bark like a dog or laugh like a crazy man. His eyes shone like burning coals, and when he was annoyed he might go so far as to set the barn on fire.

One can see from these descriptions that household spirits are much the same from Ireland to Russia. That is partly because that whole area is inhabited by peoples whose languages and legends belong to the so-called Indo-European family. That is to say that their cultures and languages have certain things in common which make them more like each other than they are like those of other groups such as the Sino-Tibetan of the Far East, the Hamito-Semitic of the Near East, the Niger-Congo of Africa, or the Algonquian of North America. (There are many more.)

It is apparent that a similar process occurred in many of the Indo-European mythologies, for we find that some of the Little People we have just discussed were once gods, just like the Faery Folk. In course of time, when the pagan religions were replaced by Christianity, the deities who had been looked to as protectors of houses and barns reappeared in folklore. Traditions like these often linger on for a long time, even after people become a little ashamed of them because they "know better." As an Irishman is supposed to have remarked, "Of course we don't believe in the Little People—*but they still exist, you know.*"

Sometimes folk beliefs are influenced by what might be called imported gods. If we remember that the Romans once occupied most of western Europe except Scandinavia it may help to explain the Brownie. Every Roman family had a special deity known as the Lar, who was actually more ancient than the major gods, such as Jupiter and Juno. The Lar's altar was the hearth, and his rough image was usually carved from a tree stump, so that he must have appeared remarkably like a little, gnarled brown man. Each family's Lar looked after its household affairs in a way that should sound very familiar to us by now. Some scholars have thought that the Lar brought to England by the Romans was the direct ancestor of the Hob, who is sometimes called the Lob. Perhaps the Brownie is a sort of combination of a Lar and a Pixie.

Lest we think that belief in mischievous little people has died out entirely in modern times, we should give a thought to the Gremlins. These little characters were invented as recently as World War I, when Allied pilots began to identify Gremlins as the cause of any otherwise untraceable mechanical troubles in their planes. During World War II it became understood that the wives of Gremlins were called Fifinellas and their young were Widgets. One and all they shared a passion for drinking aviation gasoline and were thus the cause of many dangerous fuel shortages. Luckily, however, all varieties of Gremlin were terrified of carrier pigeons, wherefore some pilots thought it advisable to carry pigeons with them if the presence of Gremlins was suspected.

Though Gremlins are plainly related to Goblins in some way, they are not so much evil as pesky and annoying. They are a perfect demonstration of the fact that human beings cannot resist the temptation to blame their problems on someone or something else.

Not all of the world's many tribes of Little People associate with the human race. In fact the Dwarfs, who are the best known of the group, hardly ever go near a house or village if they can help it. But in spite of their exclusiveness we know a good deal about Dwarfs and their life, mainly from Teutonic myths and tales in which they play large roles.

At heart, all Dwarfs are underground folk. They belong deep in rock and earth, at the roots of the mountains, and though they sometimes have to come above ground, they are never really comfortable except in their own caverns. The seven Dwarfs whom Snow White met were quite exceptional in living in a cottage in the woods, even though they spent their time in the typical Dwarfish activity of mining. If there is one thing Dwarfs love more than a good deep cave it is the precious metals and jewels that their constant digging uncovers.

In appearance Dwarfs are unmistakable. Never more than four feet tall they are brawny and tough as old tree roots. Though their faces are pale from being underground, they are strong and vigorous. They have large heads, barrel chests, bowed legs, and sometimes pot bellies from drinking too much beer, for which they have a Germanic fondness. Dwarfs are almost always bearded, which helps to give them their usual appearance of age. One hardly ever hears of a young Dwarf and peculiarly enough there are *no* female Dwarfs. That is a very odd circumstance indeed. Giants and Trolls certainly have wives, Mermaids mate with Mermen, and Witches can be either male or female. As for Faery women and Ogresses, they are almost more numerous than their men. But Dwarfs are bachelors.

A rather unappealing myth about the creation of the Teutonic world says that the first Dwarfs were grubs that appeared in the corpse of the slain Jotun Ymir, mentioned in Chapter I. From these grubs the gods formed rational beings and ordained that they should continue to burrow in the flesh of the dead Giant after it was transformed into the Earth. When a Dwarf was killed he was to be replaced by the agency of two Magician princes instead of being born from females in the usual way. Like many mythical "explanations," this one has the drawback of leaving us no better informed than we began.

Maybe it is their lack of home life that has given Dwarfs their gruff personalities. They are not very talkative, and they will stand no nonsense from anyone, especially anyone taller. Like human beings some Dwarfs are good and some are not, but even the kindest ones conceal their feelings beneath a rough exterior. No one makes a more steadfast and loyal ally than a good Dwarf, while there is no more determined and cunning enemy than a bad one.

When Dwarfs turn to evil deeds it is probably because they have given way to the major passion of all their people: the mining and working of precious metals. Dwarfs are the greatest miners in the world, and their tunnels go to fabulous depths. In its best form their love of gold is an artistic one. They are without rivals as jewelers and metalsmiths, and their work is famed for its magical properties as well as for its beauty. However, some Dwarfs lose sight of their artistic pride and become misers, wishing only to gather greater and greater hoards of treasure. They can become addicted to gold the way a human being can to drink or drugs (or gold, for that matter) and then there is no stopping them.

In Teutonic mythology the Dwarfs supplied the gods with some of their greatest treasures and weapons. It was they, for example, who made the magical chain that was used to bind the monster-wolf Fenris, who was so powerful he threatened the whole world. The chain was composed of six magical materials: the mew of a cat, the beard of a woman, the roots of a mountain, the tendons of a bear, the breath of a fish, and the spittle of a bird.

Other famous Dwarf-made objects were the god Thor's thunderbolt hammer, a golden arm ring which multiplied itself every nine days, and Skidbladnir, the ship of the gods, which was so cunningly made that it could fold up into pocket size, yet would carry all the gods over sea or land when opened. The Dwarfs are also responsible for the manufacture of all the best magical swords. Many Dragons and Giants of the old tales would still be around today if the heroes who slew them had not been so well armed.

The Dwarfs have many close relatives in other parts of the world. In Scandinavia they are called Gnomes and are almost the same in every way except that, like the Slavik Ovinniks, they have cats' whiskers and glowing red eyes. The Gnomes sometimes live with Trolls and manufacture treasures for them. There is a legend of one Troll, for example, who had a gold and silver bed quilt, which you may be sure was not made by any Troll-wife. At other times Gnomes come near enough to men to live in barns and stables. Unlike the Dwarfs, who usually dress in leather with red caps or miner's hats, the Gnomes wear gray. They are a little more friendly than Dwarfs, but not much.

In Cornwall there are said to be some little folk in the tin mines who call themselves Knockers. According to some, they are the spirits of a group of Jews who were forced to work in the mines very long ago. Whoever they are, they are friendly to other miners, and their tapping warns of dangerous cave-ins or points out rich veins of ore.

Other parts of England are inhabited by the Yarthkins, whose name implies they are "little men of the earth." They are the size of a one-year-old child and very hairy. According to one account, they are the color of "fresh-turned earth in the spring." Little more is known of them except that their gifts are unlucky to receive.

Moving west across the Atlantic we find a great many beings of the Dwarf type among the mythologies of North and South America. The Eskimos recognize a little woman called the Tootega, who lives on an island in a stone house and can walk on water. The legends do not say so, but perhaps the Tootega walks to land in order to visit the little man named Eeyeekalduk, who has a jet-black face and who lives inside a stone. In spite of the fact that it is dangerous to look into Eeyeekalduk's eyes, he is friendly to man and often heals the sick. Another Eskimo Dwarf spirit is the unpronounceable Kingmingoarkulluk, unusual among the Little People in that he is so overjoyed to be seen by a human being that he bursts into song whenever it happens.

The Iroquois divide the Little People into three groups. The Ga-hongas live in water and rocks; the Gandayaks take care of green plants and the fish in the rivers; and the Ohdowas live underground and are in charge of monsters and all kinds of venomous creatures.

Among the many small but dangerous beings to be found in the mythologies of South and Central America are the Aztec Tepictoton, Dwarfs said to be the protectors of the mountains. The Tepictoton were so much feared that children were sacrificed to appease their anger, a not uncommon feature of Aztec religion.

Many Japanese rivers have been haunted by the Dwarf Kappa. He was an evil fellow who liked to drown travelers. His power came from

61

the magic water that filled his skull, and it was by knowing that fact that one could overcome him. Kappa, it seems, was very polite and if one bowed to him he would have to return the courtesy, thus spilling out the magic water. After that he was harmless, and the river might safely be crossed.

The ancient Egyptians had a Dwarf god whose name was Bes. Stone statues show him with a large head, huge eyes, hairy chin, round cheeks, and protruding tongue. Bes usually wears an ostrich-feather headdress and a leopard skin. Inscriptions say he came from the land of Punt (probably the East African area that is now the Somali Republic). Why this rather rowdy fellow, who is often shown dancing or fighting, should have been worshiped as the protector of marriage and the affairs of women is something of a mystery. He was also the guardian of sleep and of wild beasts.

Although Slavic mythology has little to say of underground folk like the true Dwarfs, it does describe protective beings of other kinds for whom the vast forests and fields of Russia were natural homes. One of the strangest was the Leshy. Although usually pictured as a tiny man, the Leshy was supposed to have the disconcerting habit of changing size with the height of the trees he walked through. He could be as tall as a pine or as small as a clump of grass. His skin was an odd color because his blood was blue, while his eyes and beard were as green as the trees he ruled. The Leshy wore a red sash, but the rest of his clothing was eccentric: he did up all his buttons backward and wore his shoes on the wrong feet.

The Leshy's favorite pastime was to lead travelers down the wrong path in his forest. However, he was basically good-natured and would eventually lead them back home if they knew the proper way to escape his spell. To do this the travelers had to sit down, remove all their clothes, and put them on again backward, not forgetting to wear the shoes on the wrong feet.

The only exceptions to the Leshy's good humor were likely to occur in springtime, when he suffered a sort of seasonal madness. The reason was that the whole tribe of Leshies disappeared or temporarily died in October, with the falling of the leaves, and their annual reappearance left them touchy and irritable, like snakes which have just shed their skin, or animals in the mating season. Then the Leshy would run through the forest making a hideous noise—a sobbing, laughing, whistling, shouting, and birdlike shrieking all at once. At those times it was better to stay far away from him.

Just as every forest was thought to have its Leshy, every field had its Polevik. This being could appear in several shapes, the least startling of which was simply that of someone dressed in white. More often, the Polevik was either a deformed Dwarf who spoke human language or a little man with a body as brown as earth and eyes of two different colors.

The Polevik, like the Leshy, used to enjoy misleading travelers. He would also become enraged at laziness and sometimes went so far as to strangle farm workers who had gotten drunk and gone to sleep instead of working. A neglected field was a great worry to the Polevik, and he would send his children to catch the birds who stole the grain. The young Poleviks were very good at this task, bringing the birds to their parents to eat.

There is one other tribe of Little People to be considered before ending this discussion. Because most people think they are almost indistinguishable from the Pixies and Faeries, you may wonder why the Elves have not been mentioned before. Elves, however, are quite separate from these others. The word "Elf" was brought into English from the Germanic languages by the Saxons, and it originally meant *any* kind of supernatural being. Elves in the oldest Teutonic myths sound much like the true Faery Folk, but in the folklore of their native lands (especially Scandinavia) they most often appear in the form of Light Elves. They were perhaps the smallest of the Little People, being less than a foot high. Bright and shining, they had the gauzy wings and gentle ways later attributed to the Faeries and Pixies. The confusion was made easier when the English word "Elf" began to be applied to the smallest variety of the helpful, moon-dancing Pixies. Swedish tales of the Light Elves often described them as sitting on flowers, conversing with birds and doing the other picturesque things that led many writers of the last century (particularly writers of children's stories) to believe that Elves were cute. What was often forgotten or ignored was that the Light Elves were not feather-headed fantastics whose only purpose was to flit from flower to flower. In the early myths—and the Light Elves are at least as old in them as the Dwarfs and the Trolls—they were protective nature spirits like the Leshy.

Without the Light Elves, it was once believed, the whole natural world would go out of tune. Flowers would fail to bloom and set their seed, birds to sing their mating songs or lay their eggs, the salmon to swim up the rivers to spawn. The power of the Light Elves was the force of the seasons, bringing each thing to birth, growth, and death in its own time. It is a measure of how far the old traditions have been forgotten that Peter Pan's Tinkerbelle (who is a Light Elf if she is anything) could be portrayed in the Walt Disney movie as a self-centered and pouting little doll in a sort of bathing suit. This is the point at which the Little People come full circle to the misconceptions mentioned at the beginning of Chapter II.

If we now ask our recurring question: Did the Little People really exist? the surprising answer is: Yes, of course. That is to say it is not even very unusual to find human beings who are far below average size. First of all, there are today several tribes of people called pygmies, whose adult height normally varies from five feet, three inches, down to four feet, seven and a half inches. There are pygmies living in equatorial Africa, southeast Asia, the Philippine Islands and other places. They don't differ from the rest of humanity in any way except that they are of small stature.

History makes it plain that there must once have been even more pygmy tribes, which have now disappeared. Homer, for instance, was aware of the existence of a pygmy people of Upper Egypt, who called themselves the Akka, and it can hardly be that such tales had no effect on belief in the various kinds of legendary Little People. Nevertheless, even at that time most pygmy tribes were found in remote places, so that their existence was a matter of rumor only.

There is a second kind of very small person, however, who was known in every part of the world. It is a fact of biology that some children of ordinary-sized parents simply fail to grow as a result of the misfunctioning of certain glands. The individuals so affected may never reach a height beyond four feet and are then called midgets, just as those whose glands have over-functioned are called giants. There are hundreds, perhaps thousands of midgets in the world at any given time, and they are exactly like the rest of us in body formation, intelligence, and so on. Midgets may even marry persons of normal height and have full-sized children.

Unfortunately, man has the nasty trait of making fun of those who are different, and there have been many times in history when midgets were persecuted or made pets of, forced to entertain the rich and powerful, and even exchanged as presents. Probably the most famous midget of recent years was Charles Sherwood Stratton, who was born in Bridgeport, Connecticut, in 1832. He became known to the world under the management of showman P.T. Barnum as General Tom Thumb. Stratton's adult height was three feet, four inches, and he was by no means the smallest midget on record.

A third kind of very small human being is called, to make things confusing, a dwarf. Real dwarfs are anywhere from two to four feet tall, like midgets, but in contrast to them are not proportioned like other people. Though the matter is not always so simple, in general the small size of midgets results from a malfunction of the pituitary gland, while that of dwarfs is caused by both the pituitary and the thyroid. As a result dwarfs frequently have bodies of normal size but very short limbs and large heads. Though these real dwarfs are thus somewhat like the Dwarfs of legend and must have contributed to ideas about them and the god Bes, they are as truly human as giants, pygmies, midgets and ourselves, the ones in the middle.

So far, we have discussed some real human beings who could have influenced the formation of the legends by confirming a general idea that not everybody is the same size. To take the investigation further brings us once again into the field of anthropology. The following is a description of a being which could easily double as a Pixie or a Brownie:

> Kalanoro is a little land dwarf, which is not more than two feet high, entirely covered with long hair and is the wife of another dwarf called Kotokely; Kalanoro lives in caves where she lies on a fairy's bed made of silkworm cocoons. She is interested in the children of men, stealing them and substituting her own young; she makes the babies she has stolen drink special potions which prevent them from growing. Ill-favoured new-born children are sometimes called 'sons of Kalanoro,' and in the country the parents keep careful watch at a birth to see that Kalanoro does not succeed in making an exchange.
>
> Around Lake Kinkony the Sakalava have a very different notion of the Kalanoro. This rather more masculine creature lives in the thickets and reeds on the edges of lagoons. It is less than three feet high; it has long hair and only three toes on its feet. It has a sweet woman's voice, lives on fish and raw food, and walks in the country in the evening. If you meet one, it will accost you and hold you in conversation while it gradually leads you away until you disappear into the lake. Farther north on the other hand, the Kalanoro lives in woods and caves, and does not try to lead human beings astray, but it has hooked nails with which it can give cruel wounds to anyone who tries to capture it; it lives on milk, which it sometimes comes and steals even from the natives' huts. In short, young and old fear the Kalanoro, whose name parents invoke to make their children keep quiet.*

All in all, the baby-snatching, milk-stealing, hairy little Kalanoro who misleads travelers could not sound more familiar. There is only one

*Quoted from Raymond Decary by Bernard Heuvelmans in his book, *On the Track of Unknown Animals* (London: Hill & Wang, Paladin Books, 1965), pp. 322-323.

67

trouble. The account comes from Madagascar, an island off the east coast of Africa, which is very far indeed from Pixie and Brownie country. At the very least, the Kalanoro provides fascinating proof of the worldwide similarity of various legendary beings. But what if the Kalanoro were based on a real creature, as Dr. Bernard Heuvelmans has suggested in his utterly fascinating book. Even then, we would have to determine how or whether accounts of it could have reached the peoples of northern Europe, or possibly their remote ancestors elsewhere, though it is very risky to rely on transmission of legendary material over such long periods.

First let us see exactly what Dr. Heuvelmans thinks of the Kalanoro stories. He points out that there is undoubted fossil evidence that there survived in Madagascar until quite recently several species of giant lemurs—giants, that is, by the standards of this type of primate which usually ranges in size from four inches to three feet. One of these supposedly extinct lemurs is called *hadropithecus*, and was certainly alive and well in the fairly recent past, since the remains of it were not yet fossilized (replaced by minerals) when discovered. *Hadropithecus* was remarkable for the generally human shape of its skull, even though the lemurs belong to a branch of the primate family that is somewhat less advanced (that is, less like man) than either the monkeys or the apes. If it were alive today or recently enough extinct so that the Malagasy people remembered it in their tales, there is no reason why *hadropithecus* should not have been very much like the Kalanoro—a little hairy being with a human profile who sometimes lived in caves and stole food. It is also true that several of the living lemurs have long nails with which they can scratch and gouge very effectively. And lest we think that Madagascar is too small a place to hide an unknown animal, we should remember that it is the third largest island in the world and has been estimated to hold eight or nine million acres of virgin forest. If *hadropithecus* were someday to be found alive there we might discover why baby-stealing is so often a part of the story of the Little People, since none of the known apes or monkeys seems at all interested in adopting human children. At present, however, we must admit that the connection of Kalanoro with *hadropithecus* is only speculation.

Madagascar is not the only site of tales about little hairy men. From many places on the African mainland there have come reports of creatures called the agogwe, described by one hunter as "the little furry men whom one does not see once in a lifetime." Bands of these agogwe have sometimes chased men from their territory with great determination, throwing rocks and other missiles. In general the descriptions agree that the agogwe are about four feet tall, that their hair is reddish, and that there is some difficulty in judging whether they behave more like advanced apes or very primitive men. For example, one informant asserted that his father was once stunned by the little men when he incautiously entered a strange cave. On coming to, he found that his captors had not bothered to take away his spear, as if they were unaware of the use of any weapon except teeth, hands, and stones for throwing.

Dr. Heuvelmans points out that once again there is a creature known from its remains and assumed to be extinct that could easily fit the descriptions of the agogwe—the *australopithecus*, a creature of about four feet tall who looked rather like an upright-walking chimpanzee, but whose shorter arms, straighter legs, and flatter chest were

more like those of a man. Fossil evidence from Africa and elsewhere shows that *australopithecus* was living as recently as 500,000 years ago, and many scientists believe he was contemporary with man in those areas and was perhaps killed off by his larger and brighter fellow primate.

What is true of *hadropithecus* in Madagascar is even more true of *australopithecus* in Africa—there is plenty of unknown territory for him to be lost in. At the same time, there is no material evidence whatsoever to indicate that *australopithecus* is not extinct—unless one counts the tales of the agogwe.

The same thing applies to other unexplained stories of little men, particularly those of the orang pendek of Sumatra, the nittaewo of Ceylon, and the maribundas of the Amazon. They are all supposed to be little hairy men and might be, could *just possibly* be, primates previously unknown or thought to exist only as fossils.

The worst difficulty with all this speculation is that it doesn't leave us much further ahead with our investigation of mythical Little People, especially those of Russia, western Europe, and North America, whence came so many of our examples. The one thing no one has suggested is that there are apes, ape-men, or monkeys in any of those places, with the one exception of the American sasquatch mentioned in connection with the Giants and the yeti. The fact is that all primates other than man live in warm, usually tropical climates. For one reason, they have not yet learned to wear clothes, and for another, they live by hunting and gathering their food from the plants and animals that flourish year-round in warm places, but which are not available during the winter, even in the so-called temperate regions. It is not possible to say whether the striking resemblance of some of the Little People to those creatures from tropical regions described in purportedly true tales is anything more than coincidence.

We cannot end this chapter without a brief mention of the so-called Cottingley Faeries. The name refers to a most intriguing account of two girls who claimed to have *photographed*, in 1917, some of the beings often called Faeries, classed here more exactly as Elves or Pixies.

The children involved were ten-year-old Frances Griffiths and her thirteen-year-old cousin, Elsie Wright, whose family Frances was visiting in Cottingley, England. Elsie's parents thought the two girls were merely being imaginative when they reported playing with "Faeries" in the wooded glen near the Wrights' house. To prove their story, Frances and Elsie persuaded Mr. Wright to lend them his new camera. There was only one plate in the camera, after the fashion of 1917, and when the girls brought it back and Elsie's father developed it, he saw what certainly looked like a group of Elves or Sprites (a word for spirits in general) dancing in front of Frances.

The parents suspected that the girls had faked the photograph with cut-out paper, but found no evidence of paper snippings when they went to the glen to investigate. Accordingly, Mr. Wright allowed Frances and Elsie to use another plate a few days later, and the second picture showed Elsie with a little winged creature stepping onto her knee.

Interestingly enough, the Wrights seem to have dismissed the affair from their minds for three years—until Mrs. Wright attended a lecture by the well-known spiritualist Edward L. Gardner, who mentioned that many persons were interested in the possibility of spirit photographs.

From this point on, the story is a matter of interpreting the competence of expert witnesses. The photographs were examined by a variety of knowledgeable specialists, some of whom declared them to be genuine, and none of whom could prove they were fakes. The defense of the Cottingley Faeries was eventually taken up by no less famous a person than author Sir Arthur Conan Doyle, whose interest in spiritualism and the occult was well known. Gardner, Conan Doyle, and another believer in spiritualism, Mr. Geoffrey Hudson, held that Frances was a medium (a person through whom, some believe, the spirit world can communicate with the real one), and that the gauzy beings in the pictures were formed of ectoplasm. That point of view, of course, replaces one mystery with another, for we know even less about such reported psychic phenomena than we do about folklore and prehistory. Nevertheless, the photographs caused quite a stir in their time, although modern psychical investigators have declared them to be obvious fakes. The major objection to the Cottingley pictures from the vantage point of the folklorist is that the "Faeries" they show are so inauthentic in appearance. Not only do they have many of the features of the prettified nineteenth-century stories, but they are shown, in three more photographs which Frances took in 1920 at the request of Dr. Gardner, to be wearing the bobbed hair and short skirts which were just then coming into fashion. They simply don't look like genuine Elves, and even less like Pixies or Faeries. If the Little People are going to turn out to be psychic phenomena, as many spiritualists believe, it would be reasonable to think they would retain some of the magical and even awesome traits that are theirs in the oldest tales and traditions.

IV
WORKERS OF EVIL—AND A FEW GOOD SPIRITS

*In what revolting fancy were the Forms begot
Of all these monsters?*

—Aldous Huxley

WE HAVE ALREADY SEEN that some of the Impossible People were born because their creators needed to explain the mysterious and sometimes frightening world. The Titans and Jotuns, for example, represented earthquakes, storms, volcanic eruptions, and other natural events.

In the same way most of the mythologies of the world contain tales of beings whose only purpose is to help the forces of evil or good that shape men's lives. These spirits are good or evil all the time, all the way through. That is generally not so of the other Impossible People. Even Ogres don't spend their days *trying* to do evil. Their only desire is to catch a nice fat human being for dinner, and it is only an accident that the human beings object to this behavior. As for the Giants, Dwarfs,

Faery Folk, Brownies, and so on, we have seen that they can be both helpful and harmful, just like most human beings. But the spirits we are about to discuss have only one nature. They work twenty-four hours a day at their jobs, though for some reason it is the evil ones about whom we hear most.

The commonest name for an evil spirit is Demon or Devil, although the situation is complicated by the fact that in ancient Greece *Daimon* was a general name for any spirit and one still occasionally finds the word used in that sense. Since there is hardly anywhere in the world where Demons do not appear in some form we shall only be able to mention a few of them here.

Among the complex and varied mythologies of Africa, that of the East African Nandi people provides one of the most fearsome Demons anywhere. The Chemosit, as he is called, not only eats human beings, but is said to prefer children to adults. He is half man and half bird, and has only one leg, but nine buttocks. His mouth shines red in the dark like a lantern, and he manages to walk with the help of a stick like a crutch. Some writers have tried to connect the Chemosit to a creature called the Nandi bear which appears persistently in local lore. However, since the Nandi bear is also believed to be mythical (at least, no one has convincingly identified it) it seems as if the Chemosit will probably continue to be classified as a Demon.

The folk tales of Arab countries are populated with beings who have become well known in the west through the *Arabian Nights*. Thus almost anyone can tell you that a Djinn (or Jinn, or Genie, as it is sometimes spelled) is an enormous spirit which can be condensed into a bottle, corked, and kept until the owner of the bottle wants a stupendous task performed or unlimited treasure brought. What is not so well understood is that the Djinn is a Demon of the worst sort. Only a very powerful Magician would dare try to shut him up in a bottle; the ordinary mortal who had such audacity would be destroyed like a gnat.

Another kind of evil spirit of the Arab world is the Afrit who can assume any form at all in order to serve his evil ends. An Afrit may look like a harmless pygmy, but he can turn in an instant into a roaring lion or a smothering sandstorm.

The Hindu mythology of India is filled with tales of Demons that are among the world's most spectacular and grotesque. It is difficult to describe Indian Demons in general because each one seems to be different, although they all share the characteristic of being perfectly hideous. Some of their most common features are horns, burning eyes, eight or a hundred arms, protruding tongues, and animal heads. If they wish to, however, Demons can look just like human beings in order to trap and confuse their victims.

An excellent description of the nature of Demons is contained in the legend of the man Daksha, who allowed his daughter to marry Siva, the Lord of the Demons, but later turned against his son-in-law, denouncing him as "this sullied personage, abolisher of rites and destroyer of boundaries," and adding, "he frequents horrible cemeteries, accompanied by crowds of spirits and ghosts, looking like a madman, naked, with disheveled hair, wearing a garland of skulls and human bones . . . a lunatic beloved of lunatics whose nature is wholly obscure."

The line between gods and Demons in the Brahmanic tradition of India is not an uncrossable one, and it is interesting to note in this connection that the same beings who are described as Demons in India

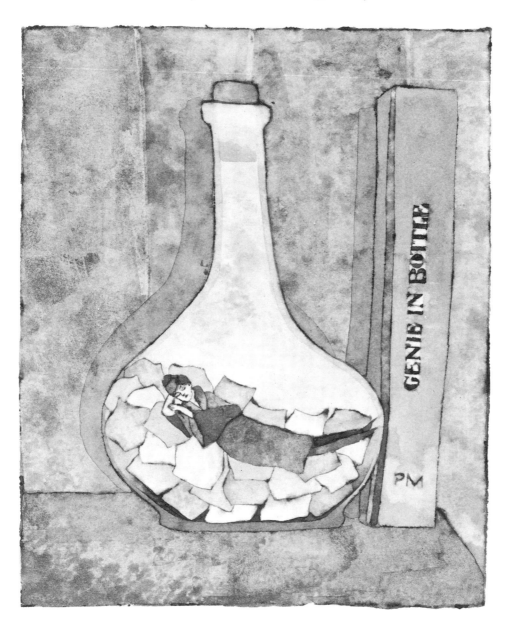

were gods in ancient Persia. The story of the Demon Ravana tells how one day a very holy being in the heaven of the god Vishnu committed a serious error. The punishment was to return to earth to regain spiritual merit. Offered a choice of living through three incarnations (other lives) as the enemy of Vishnu or seven incarnatons as the god's friend, the sinner chose the former path as the quickest and became thereby the Demon Ravana, whose three successive lives are doomed to end in death at the hand of Vishnu, after which he will return to heaven.

The evil spirits of Chinese mythology sound surprisingly like the Devils of European tradition. They are the helpers of the eighteen Yama-Kings who rule over hell. Pictures show the Chinese Devils with two lumps on their foreheads, which are meant to be horns. These Devils are bare to the waist (because of the hot climate in which they work) and carry iron-spiked maces or tridents. Many of these features were carried eastward to China from India just as they also traveled westward to influence our own ideas of Devils, at least in their most common form.

Those familiar beings, haunters of westerners' nightmares, may be huge and powerful or small and ugly. In either case, Devils have horns on their heads like those of goats and long hairless tails with hooks on the ends. Their ears are pointed and from the waist down they have the haunches, hocks, and cloven hoofs of the goat. Sometimes they also have bat's wings. They may be fat or thin, but they usually wear short pointed beards, have upward slanting eyebrows, and dress in red or black when they bother with human clothing. Devils do not usually wear clothes except in the upper world; at home in hell they only carry a pitchfork.

Devils sometimes try very hard to disguise themselves as human beings in order to deceive the unwary. However, an observant person can always find some sign of a Devil's true nature—a hoof mark where there should have been a footprint, perhaps, or a pair of eyes glowing green in the dark like a cat's. In earlier pictures the Devil is not nearly so suave and refined as the gentleman in the red-lined opera cape with whom most of us are familiar. The fact that Devils are partly animal in appearance shows that their behavior is also partly animal. They can be gross, brutal, and vicious in a completely inhuman way. It does not do to take Devils too lightly, for they are masters of lying, disguise, and trickery. They love war and terror, suffering and injustice, and in one sense the truth about Devils is that they are in all of us because they represent the worst side of human nature.

Imps are not usually supposed to be as bad as Devils, but they are quite bad enough. Sources disagree about whether Imps stay Imps all their lives or whether they get to be Devils when they grow up. In either case, they look rather like Devils except that they are smaller and uglier. They are usually the color of boiling pitch or glowing coals, and though their evil deeds are limited to nasty tricks and mean-spirited practical jokes, one gets the impression that they would like to go on to bigger and worse evils if they were able.

"Fiend" is generally considered to be just another word for Devil. If it is possible to tell the two beings apart it may be because in folktales Fiends seem to be less subtle. Devils may use charm and persuasion in putting their evil propositions. Fiends, on the other hand, hate human beings so much that they don't bother to pretend otherwise. (The name

Fiend comes from roots in Old English and Icelandic meaning "the enemy" and also "to hate.") Fiends don't contrive elaborate plots and schemes; they just like to go out and hurt people.

In medieval times the artists who painted the Devils and their helpers on manuscripts or carved them in stone got many of their ideas from the sculptures found in Roman ruins. It seems quite likely that the image of Devils was partly derived from that of the classical Satyrs, little fellows half goat and half man of whom more will be said in the next chapter. The ancient Hebrew custom of sacrificing a goat to atone for the sins of the people was probably also a factor in giving the Devil his goatlike features. This sacrificed goat, from which we derive the term scapegoat, became a symbol of evil which it later seemed natural to associate with the Devil, the Evil One. Other aspects of the Devil's appearance will be discussed later when we consider his role as the horned god worshipped by Witches.

Thus far in our discussion of western Devils we have been speaking mainly of ideas that were popular in folklore. However, there appeared during the medieval period a great deal of material concerned with the serious, scholarly study of the supposed habits and history of Devils. This branch of learning, generally called Demonology, presents an altogether different picture of Devils than was current among the less educated. According to this view, the rulers of hell were distinguished by rank and title very much as were the rulers of Europe at the time. There were several competing versions of this organization, each assigning different names and functions to the various infernal rulers. In one of the most complete and specific descriptions the next most important Devils after the supreme ruler Satan are said to be the kings of the

80

four principal regions—Zimimar, King of the North; Gorson, King of the South; Amaymon, King of the East; and Goap, King of the West. Subordinate to the Devil Kings are innumerable Dukes, Marquises, Counts, Earls, Knights, Presidents, and Prelates of hell, each of whom has certain duties and commands certain legions. The number of Devils in those legions was variously estimated at 133,306,668 in 1459 by Alphonsus de Spina and at a more conservative 7,405,926 by the sixteenth-century Demonologist Johan Weyer. According to Weyer the supreme monarch of the hellish host is Beelzebub rather than Satan, who is demoted to the position of Chief of the Opposition. Other major figures are Moloch, Chief of the Army; Pluto, Prince of Fire; Leonard, Grand Master of the Sphere; Adramelech, Grand Chancellor; Astaroth, Grand Treasurer; Nergal, Chief of the Secret Police; and Baal, Chief of the Satanic Army (the latter presumably next under Moloch).

By the time of Weyer, each of these chief Devils and their cohorts had been given individual physical descriptions and it is clear that they were by no means merely copies of Satan or Beelzebub himself. To take a few examples at random from the beginning of one alphabetical list, there was the Devil Agares, who appeared as a lord mounted on a crocodile and carrying a hawk on his fist, commanding thirty-one legions. Amon, a marquis commanding forty legions, took the shape either of a wolf with a serpent's tail vomiting flame or of a man with an owl's head bearing fangs. Bael sported the heads of a cat, a crab, and a man and held lands in the eastern region of hell. Balan also had three heads, those of a bull, a man, and a ram. His eyes burned with fire, he had the tail of a serpent, and he rode on a bear. Others of the Devil's followers had such features as a dog's teeth with a raven's head or a lion's head, a goose's feet, and a hare's tail. In these respects they sound much like the Demons of India and the Near East, and this fact is not surprising since in their search for knowledge of Devils the medieval scholars drew heavily on the older Jewish and Muslim traditions that were themselves derived from even more ancient sources in Babylonia and Persia. We have already seen how the gods of one religion become the Demons and lesser spirits of the cult that replaces them, so it is natural that the names of many Devils were once those of pagan gods such as Baal, Amon, Moloch, Pluto, and Astaroth.

It is plain from what has been said above that Demons and Devils in western mythology are primarily beings of another world, usually the world of the dead, or hell. They are not bound by the laws of time and space, which is why they seem, from the human point of view, to be able to appear and disappear or change shape at will.

By no means all of the evil beings in European folklore are specifically associated with the underworld, however. One old English Demon of the upper regions was Mara, who, like her colleagues in hell, took her name from that of a pagan goddess. Not much is known about Mara's appearance, but it can't have been pleasant, for from her name are derived the terms "nightmare" and "mare's nest." She was supposed to carry her victims off in their sleep.

The fear of being snatched away is a widespread one, and there are all kinds of Things in folklore which, like the Gobble-uns of Little Orphan Annie, will "git you ef you dont watch out." The Goblins themselves were derived from the same roots as the Kobolds (one can see that the names are similar). The Kobolds of Germany, as we said earlier, were nothing more than extra-mischievous Brownies, with perhaps a greater tendency to steal things. In Britain the Goblins started out much the same way. It was only in the seventeenth and eighteenth centuries, when England and Scotland were seized with an almost panic fear of Witches that many persons were frightened into believing that all mythical beings were agents of the Devil. At that time the Goblins somehow changed forever and became thoroughly wicked.

In appearance Goblins vary from small to near human size. Sometimes they *look* almost human from a distance, but those who claim to have examined them up close say they are merely clumsy and grotesque imitations of human beings. As if someone had tried to build them from an incomplete set of blueprints, they are always deformed in some upsetting way. Their eyelids may close from the bottom up, or they may have seven fingers, no ears, three rows of teeth, no joints in their arms and legs. They also have speech impediments unlike any of those that afflict real human beings. Their voices have been described as "weak, small, whispering, and imperfect."

Surely a relative of the Goblins and Devils is the Krampus. In Austria this horned and furry figure was said to be the Christmastime companion of jolly Saint Nicholas. While Saint Nick gave presents to good children, it was the Krampus who left lumps of coal or sticks and stones for the bad ones.

A totally different sort of creature is the Hag, who should not be confused either with the Witch or with just any mean old woman. In legend, Witches are human beings with special powers, while Hags are supernatural malignant spirits. Hags appear as hideous females of great age, with bent backs, rheumy eyes, clawlike hands, sunken cheeks, long noses, wispy hair, and sometimes pointed teeth. One of the most powerful of the sisterhood is called the Cailleach Bheur or "Blue Hag" of Scotland. This dreadful dame seems to represent winter. She carries a staff that freezes the earth wherever it strikes, and she can only be conquered by the springtime. Then, it is said, she flings down her staff in a rage and disappears until fall. Whin and holly bushes, under which grass never grows, mark the spots where the Cailleach Bheur casts down her staff.

Another Hag is Black Annis, who has a blue face and only one eye. Until it was filled up, a cave in the Dane Hills, England, was said to be her home. From there she would prowl the countryside in search of lambs and children to eat. It has been said that she and another Hag called Gentle Annie (who was anything but gentle) reflect memories of the Celtic goddess Danu from whom the Faery Tuatha De Danann took their name. Danu, who was sometimes called Anu, probably resembled most of the Celtic goddesses in having three aspects, or three alternate forms. (In fact, worship of triple goddesses is found in all the Indo-European mythologies.) The three forms of these goddesses are the maiden, the mother, and the crone, which is to say they represent the three phases of a woman's life span. Thus it is very interesting to learn that Hags are not always ugly, bent, and horrible. Some, like the Cailleach Bheur, are supposed to be able to appear as lovely young girls, as if they still remembered the times when they were triple goddesses.

Tales from Ireland and the Scottish highlands are full of another kind of female spirit, the Banshee. Originally, the word Banshee meant simply a Faery woman, which is the translation of the name from the Gaelic. However, the Banshee eventually got herself a reputation that sets her apart from the Faeries. By far the best-known characteristic of the Banshee is her wailing voice, which is supposed to be an omen of death to all who hear it. The Banshee is much feared for that reason, which is rather unfair because the Banshee means to be sympathetic. The classic type of Banshee attaches herself to a particular family and wails only to warn of the death of one of its members. She has no interest at all in strangers, and her wailing is a prophecy, not a cause of death. A Banshee is very loyal and has been known to follow her family when it emigrated to the New World. She has long, streaming hair and often wears a gray cloak over a green dress. Some Banshees are quite beautiful, although their eyes are always fiery red with weeping.

In Scotland the Banshee is sometimes called the Washer at the Ford, because one may find her washing the clothes of those who are about to die in battle. If you can sneak up on the Washer and catch hold of her, she will be forced to tell you the name of the doomed man and to grant you three wishes. However, it takes some courage to catch hold of this kind of Banshee, since she has only one nostril, one large projecting front tooth, and webbed feet.

Some beings are malignant toward man only because he threatens something they protect. Greek myths speak of the Oreads, a kind of Nymph whose particular charge was the mountains and grottoes. Like the Water Nymphs from whom they were derived (see Chapter VI), they were beautiful, immortal girls. The Oreads would lead travelers astray if they wandered into forbidden territory and would occasionally even push a man over a cliff. Their sisters the Dryads were Forest Nymphs who carried axes to protect the trees they guarded. Some of the Forest Nymphs were so bound up with the existence of the trees that they became almost part of them, their hair turning to leaves, and their arms to branches. They were distinguished from the other Dryads by being called Hamadryads.

There is some resemblance to the Dryads in the Celtic tree spirits who are spoken of in Britain. Among them is the One with the White Hand. Her home is Somerset, where there are many legends of walking trees. Though she possesses a Faery-like beauty, the One with the White Hand is far more terrifying than even the greatest Faery lord. They say that at twilight she will rise out of a grove of birches to follow any late traveler. Her clothes rustle like dead leaves and her face is as pale as birch bark, as pale as death, while her long hands are like blasted branches. Her touch on the head brings madness; her touch on the heart brings death.

Rather similar is the Brown Man of the Moors, whose province is the heathery hills of the English border country. The Brown Man is dangerous to human beings who trespass into his wild territory, especially those who come to hunt the game or catch the fish.

Scotland is the home of a whole host of nasty beings, most of whose names seem to begin with B. In addition to the Boggart and the Bogle, mentioned in the last chapter, there are the Bodach, the Bugaboo, the Bugbear, the Bogle-bo, and the Bogie, apparently all variations on one another. Their names are taken from that of the Celtic god Bucca and are generally used to frighten children.

Much worse than any of the above is the Bloody Bones. This monster is rumored to have a crouching form like a rock. He is covered all over with matted hair, has pale flat eyes, and lives in dark cupboards. Like the Bodach, the Bloody Bones was invoked to make children be good, but one may suspect that he scared them into fits instead.

With such a lot of horrors arrayed against him, man is lucky to have at least a few spirits looking out for his welfare. The idea that every individual has a sort of spiritual guardian watching over him alone is a widespread one. The people of ancient Assyria believed that each person was not only protected but actually followed around by a being called the Lamassu. Winged and human-headed, the Lamassu also had the body of a bull. He must have been a very reassuring guardian, for we can see his tremendous strength and dignity from the carvings on the gate of the palace of King Sargon at Khorsabad, in modern Iraq. The Lamassu were much relied on in daily life, as is indicated by the saying of the time, "The man who has no Lamassu when he walks in the street wears a headache like a garment."

Other cultures of the Near East had similar traditions. In India we hear of the Angiras, who are called sons of the gods and fathers of humanity. Like many winged beings, they had the job of acting as intermediaries between gods and men.

The Angiras are of course related to the same traditions which produced the western ideas of Angels. The name Angel and its Hebrew counterpart Malak both mean the same thing—a messenger. The Angels, like the Angiras, exist in order to perform the will of God.

It is an odd circumstance that many persons have come to think that Angels are female and that the soul of a good person turns into an Angel when he dies. Actually, both ideas contradict such sources as the Old Testament, the Apocrypha, and the early Church Fathers. Originally, the Angels of Christian, Jewish, and Islamic tradition were, like Devils, acknowledged to belong to an entirely different order of existence. They had no physical elements in their makeup and could not be conceived of as either male or female, any more than the sunlight or the wind is male or female. They were radiant beings quite beyond human power to describe or comprehend, both stern and beautiful. The last-named quality is probably responsible for one of our misconceptions about Angels, for the earliest pictures of Angels in ancient manuscripts, carvings, and mosaics showed figures with shining faces, long hair, and flowing robes. These artistic representations were done during periods when everyone dressed in such a style. But by the nineteenth century, when men wore their hair short and had given up robes for trousers, it was easy to assume from the old pictures that Angels must all be females with long hair and dresses. Another influence on later ideas about the appearance of Angels was probably found in Greek and Roman sculptures of Nike, the goddess of victory, who always appeared as a winged woman. It is for these reasons that the gold and silver angels we hang on Christmas trees usually have pretty faces and glamorous costumes more suitable for Cinderella at the ball. As with so many of the beings in this book, Angels have been made prettier and less awesome by writers of recent centuries.

It was not always so. By the end of the medieval period scholarly researchers had divided the Angels into three groups, called hierarchies, each of which contained three orders or choirs. In the First Hierarchy were the Seraphim, the Cherubim, and the Thrones; in the Second were the Dominions, the Principalities, and the Powers; in the Third, the Virtues, the Archangels, and the Angels. Probably the various orders were thought of as differing in rank, with the Seraphim as the highest and the Angels as the lowest, but there is disagreement about this. However, early paintings and manuscripts certainly show some differences among the orders, if only in the color with which they are surrounded. Thus for example the Seraphim often have six wings and appear on a red background, while Cherubim have many heads and wings but no bodies and appear on a blue background. The various orders also performed different divine functions, according to some authorities.

The precise definitions of their duties could (and did) fill volumes, but in general the Hierarchies of Angels were in charge of maintaining the universe in its proper order. Some watched over the planets, others oversaw the sun, the stars, and the *primum mobile*, the Latin name for the forces governing the movements of heavenly bodies.

Still other Angels were concerned with human affairs. From the human point of view, Angels exhibited marvelous powers. Though pictures always show them with wings as a sign of their heavenly nature, medieval belief held that Angels did not fly like birds. That is, they did not flap their wings and did not rely on the density of the air to hold them up. Rather they were able to lift themselves at any angle and in any direction because they were superior to the law of gravity. This power is usually referred to as levitation. When need arose, Angels could move at almost miraculous speed, but it was believed they were not capable of reading minds or foretelling the future. Angels were exceedingly wise, however, because they were able to perceive reality directly, without becoming confused by emotions, appearances, and the complexities of words, as human beings are confused.

In the light of these awesome abilities, it is no wonder that mortals sometimes tried to find ways to capture the powers of the Angels (and the Devils) for themselves. Those who did so were usually known as Witches or Magicians.

It may not be entirely appropriate to include Wizards, Magicians, Sorcerers, Sorceresses, and Witches in a book on mythical beings because even when they appear in myths it is clear that their origins are human. The names listed above are applied to those who have tried, by good means or evil, to master the unknown. They are traffickers in spells, potions, lore, curses, learning, and above all, magic. Moreover, they are doubly difficult to write about because they one and all belong to fact as well as to legend.

There are many real Wizards, Magicians, and Sorcerers in the world today, even aside from the ones who make their living giving magic shows in theaters and at parties. (Witches are factual too, but we will discuss them a little later.) In the islands of the East Indies, in India, in the interior of Australia, in the Caribbean islands, in the northernmost parts of Alaska, Siberia, Canada, Russia, and Finland, in parts of Africa and even in isolated places elsewhere, there live peoples who rely on certain members of the community to insure that the powers of the unseen do not destroy them. Anthropologists often call these experts shamans, but they can equally well go by any of the names we have been discussing. Their function has been part of human life since long before the invention of writing—since the time when human beings became really human, that is, members of the species *Homo sapiens.* The earliest records of man's past are rock paintings in the Sahara Desert (once a green and fertile plain), in caves in the south of France, and in a few other places. At the time when the paintings were made there was no farming, no boat building, no city life. There was only the hunt for food, in which man pitted himself directly against the bison, the wild horse, the reindeer, or the antelope. And in the pictures the hunters made on the rocks are shown dancing figures that look like men but have certain animal features such as bison's heads or horse's tails. Though scholars are not agreed on whether the pictures represent men dressed up in costumes or mythical beings who were part animal, it is often suggested that the drawings were not done for decorative purposes, but in order to *influence* the outcome of the hunt. They are magical because they try to draw on other kinds of forces than those of day-to-day life. For example, anyone can tell the difference between a piece of paper with a rabbit drawn on it and a live rabbit. But for magical purposes there is *no* difference. The rabbit on the paper becomes the live rabbit, for pictures are as powerful in magic as names. In the magical system the picture of a thing, or its name, or even a piece of it is believed to give the possessor some control over the thing itself. The cave pictures were meant to bring the game to the hunters through the principle that like draws like. The men who made the pictures, whose portraits *may* be found in the figures in animal costume, were thus the earliest Magicians. The profession has been part of human life ever since, although the rise of civilization has brought many changes in ideas about what Magicians and their colleagues do and what they are like.

In the myths and legends of the world Magicians are human beings who have studied the supernatural and learned to control it. By muttering a spell or waving their hands, or even just thinking, they can summon powers greater than those of any king or army. They are, in short, the men of superior wisdom. In later times, when magic went out of style, Magicians were often feared and sometimes persecuted because of their activities. Together with alchemists, fortune tellers, astronomers, and others who pursued strange knowledge, they attracted the suspicion of those who knew nothing and didn't care who found it out.

Though most Magicians are only human beings with greater or

lesser degrees of alleged supernatural power, a few have become so great that legend makes them immortal, or nearly so. Even if they are not immortal, Magicians are believed to be protected by spells so that it is nearly impossible to kill them. Couple this with the fact that Magicians naturally endow themselves with long lives, and one can see why most of the clan are pictured as very old men with beards and bushy eyebrows. It is also quite correct to think of the Magician as wearing the tall pointed hat and long gown woven with strange symbols that are usually shown in portraits. The conical hat is a sort of megaphone through which he claims to receive the messages of the spirits. The symbols on the gown are magical shorthand rather like that of modern chemists and earlier alchemists.

The various names of magic-makers give us an interesting picture of their origins. A "Wizard," as the sound of the word implies, is simply a wise man. The word "Sorcerer," and of course "Sorceress," comes from the Latin *sors*, meaning fate. The Sorcerer is thus one who reads fate and can foretell the future. Magic, incidentally, is a field in which women excel, especially when the lore they study is derived from the ancient religions in which the supreme being was a goddess rather than a god. A good Sorceress knows magical secrets that are never revealed to any male Magician. The name "Magician" itself comes from that of the Magi. According to legend the wise men who visited the infant Jesus were also members of an order of Persian priests of the Zoroastrian religion. The Magi had such a reputation as spell-casters and foretellers of the future that people later thought of them as the founders of all magic, though as we have seen the practice of magic is many thousand years older than the kingdom of Persia.

Workers of Evil—and a Few Good Spirits

In contrast to all of the foregoing magic-makers who may work for either good or evil, Necromancers are always wicked. They deal exclusively in black magic, as it is sometimes called, and no good ever comes from consulting them.*

There is really no foolproof way of telling good Magicians from bad ones. The trouble is that since they are, or at least once *were* human, they share in the flaws of human nature. While good Magicians use their powers for benevolent ends and in the service of others, and while bad Magicians seek to do harm or to get wealth and power for themselves, it is always in the nature of magic to be dangerous to the user. A Magician who calls upon the powers of evil with even the best intentions often finds himself slowly corrupted by them until at last he is the servant rather than the master, doing the bidding of Demons. Magic is a lifelong study, which involves the training of the will and character as well as of the mind.

The Classical story of the Sorcerer's apprentice is a very small-scale lesson in what can happen to the unwary or overconfident person who trifles with magic. You will recall that the apprentice became tired of carrying water for the Sorcerer and, having watched him practice his spells, seized the opportunity of his master's absence to command the broom to take over his work. Here is an illustration of what might be called Rule One for magic-makers: Never start what you cannot stop. For the apprentice found that he did not know the spell

---

*At this point it should be made clear that black magic and its opposite, white magic, have nothing to do with whether those who practice them are black or white. Terms like these demonstrate and perhaps help to foster the racial prejudices that are among the worst spells mankind has cast upon itself.

that would end the fanatical broom's trips to and from the well. And when the lad tried to halt the flood by using an axe on the broom, he discovered Rule Two: Cutting a magical being in pieces causes a new one (or three, or nine, or a hundred new ones) to grow from each piece. The same principles are found in very many other tales. For instance, there is the Scandinavian story of "Why the Sea Is Salt," which tells of a woman who wished for a magic hand mill that would never run out of herring and broth. That is, of course, exactly what she got. And once the wish had been granted there was no way to turn it off. The story indicates that the hand mill is still grinding out herrings and broth to renew the world's oceans, just as the broom would still be carrying water if the Sorcerer had not returned to use the right words on it. One of the best known examples of the kill-it-and-it-multiplies theme is that of the Hydra, a nine-headed serpent that grew two new heads in place of each one cut off by the hero Herakles. Fortunately for Herakles he knew the magical solution and killed the Hydra with fire.

If it were not for certain historical accidents it would be possible to include Witches in the foregoing discussion of magic and magic-makers. They are all engaged in the same general profession and that would be the end of it except that Witches have been the subject of so much hysteria, controversy, and persecution in western society.

First let us dispose of the popular cartoon image of the Witch. We see an old woman with a long nose and warts who dresses all in black with a tall black hat and rides around the sky on a broom. She makes friends with black cats and bats, probably eats children, and her favorite night in the year is Hallowe'en. It won't be any surprise to us by now if that picture turns out to be less than the whole truth. For one thing

96

the practice of witchcraft was universally regarded as a crime as recently as two hundred years ago, and many persons were tried and executed for it. There must, then, have been a reality behind the old dame on the Hallowe'en decorations. What follows is a summary of the vast amount of material relating to real Witches and their history.

The roots of witchcraft in Europe certainly go back to pre-Christian times and some writers have suggested that they go back to the period of the paleolithic cave paintings mentioned earlier in this chapter. What seems certain is that not everyone accepted the new religion called Christianity when it was brought to Europe by missionaries during, approximately, the first eight centuries, A.D. Whether what survived was the pagan religions of the Celts, Gauls, Angles, Saxons, Teutons, Slavs, Vandals, Goths, and other tribes, or whether the cults involved were even more ancient than that, the people of Europe did not entirely abandon the old beliefs.

We have already seen how tradition said both the Faery Folk and the Trolls feared the sound of church bells, the sight of the Bible, or the touch of holy water. But the old gods and spirits didn't linger on only as folklore. In some places there was an active effort to keep alive religious ceremonies that had officially been outlawed. And simply because what they did *was* illegal, those who followed the old ways came to hate the Church and all it stood for. The members of these cults, who are the true Witches, wcrc forced to become more secretive as time went on, and to protect themselves with horror tales of what would happen to anyone who spied on their doings.

There are two separate aspects of the Witch cult. The first was the surviving bits of pre-Christian religion or religions, whose major

97

interest was the natural world. It was concerned with making the fields and flocks fertile by means of magical ceremonies and the sacrifice of animals (or occasionally human beings) to appease the wrath of the gods of the earth. (We must not overemphasize the idea of human sacrifice here. The evidence indicates that it was only the rare exception to the usual procedure.)

In all Witches' activities the central figure was that of a horned man who was either the chief Magician, like the figures in the cave paintings, or a representative of the fertility god himself. It is not really a coincidence that the Devil was also horned. Both probably had an origin similar to that of the goat-legged Satyrs, who were themselves outgrowths of ancient horned gods in Greece. At the time of the earliest true Witch cults, however, these common roots were hardly remembered, and the similarity of the Witch god to the most hated and feared figure in the Christian catalogue probably helped to bring to the Witch cult its second major aspect—one which was not merely pre-Christian or non-Christian, but decidedly anti-Christian. Over the centuries the Witches must have attracted to their ranks both those who found the old traditions too strong to give up and those who had become disillusioned with Christianity and actively wished to bring about its overthrow. It is hardly any wonder, therefore, that the Church viewed the Witches as enemies, who must at all opportunities be destroyed.

One must not imagine, however, that the members of the cult went about making spectacular claims or threats. On the contrary, most Witches were in daily life ordinary citizens of the community. A Witch might be young or old, handsome or plain, rich or poor, man or woman. And in connection with this last item, one should mention that

although many people refer to all male Witches as Warlocks, that is an error. The Warlock is an officer of the cult who has certain duties to perform at an initiation ceremony.

In any case most Witches were extremely careful to conceal their identity. Their only visible link with witchcraft would be in the form of a "familiar," whence the black cat and bat of the cartoon. In point of fact a familiar could be almost any animal, some of the most popular creatures for the post being cats (not necessarily black), toads, birds (especially owls and ravens), bats, dogs, pigs, goats, hares, mice, and even insects. Anything small enough to have around the house would do, for it was believed that the Witch could not practice magic without the help of the familiar, which was inhabited by a Demon. The familiar also carried messages to and from the Devil or other Witches and spied on the activities of the Witch's enemies.

As for wearing black, it is not likely that young and pretty female Witches would hide themselves in such somber clothes. And the tall pointed hat may have been an aid to speaking with spirits, as it was for ordinary Magicians, but was not at all essential. Most Witches dressed like anybody else in their time and place.

The one thing that separated the Witch decisively from the Magician was the requirement that the Witch make a pact with the Devil, something that most Magicians strongly denied doing. Magicians claimed to get their powers from long years of study, while Witches were given them in return for worshipping the Devil.

From the point of view of the Church, a particularly threatening fact about these worshipers of the Devil was that they were organized. Unlike the ordinary Magicians, both real and mythical, the Witches were not merely individuals engaged in forbidden researches. It was a central (in fact, *the* central) activity of Witches to gather together regularly. Local groups of Witches were called covens and usually numbered thirteen. (That is one reason why many persons consider thirteen an unlucky number.) The coven would meet once a week to carry on such business as initiating new members. These meetings were called esbats, while more important and larger gatherings were called sabbats and were held at times of the year that corresponded with the great pagan festivals of both the agricultural year (planting and harvest) and the pastoral year (the birth and mating of flocks). Two of the best-known festivals were May Eve, the last night of April; and of course Hallowe'en, the last night of October, when ghosts and Goblins are still supposed to come out to play. Other important dates were February second, the winter festival; August first, the summer festival; December twenty-first, the winter solstice; and June twenty-third, the summer solstice.

The sabbats were the source of many common ideas about Witches. It was to these festivals that Witches were supposed to fly on broomsticks. The suggestion has been made that the ointment with which the Witches undoubtedly rubbed themselves before the sabbat may have given them hallucinations of flying brought on by the powerful drugs such as aconite, belladonna, and hemlock which the ointment probably contained. Since much of what we know of the Witches comes from the confessions of those who were on trial for witchcraft, the fact that the participants *believed* themselves to have flown would be enough to start the rumor among the public. However, it is hard to guess why the broom was singled out as the favorite vehicle. Contemporary pictures of flying Witches show them riding anything from an ordinary staff or pitchfork to various animals or even nothing at all, as well as brooms. In any case, the testimony from the Witch trials makes it clear that most of the participants walked to the sabbat like anyone else.

Condensing the very varied reports of what went on at the sabbat, one finds a general picture something like this: The ceremony began at midnight (still called "the witching hour") and included food, alcoholic drink, and often magical potions containing more of the same drugs used in the ointment. It was a time for throwing off all the restraints of civilization, and for that reason can properly be termed an orgy. The next part of the festival was a wild dance, usually in a circle, which was led by some member of the cult in the mask and costume of the horned god or Devil. Excitement, exercise, drugs, and alcohol all contributed to bringing on wild outpourings of emotion, hysteria, and sometimes hallucinations. The climax of the scene was sexual intercourse among the Witches themselves or with the Horned One who led the dance. Other features might be the sacrifice of a goat or a deliberate parody of Christian religious ceremonies.

The scene just described was certainly one that would shock and horrify a stranger who happened to stumble onto it. That such observers did sometimes report on what they had seen was inevitable considering the size and loudness of the gatherings, no matter how late the hour or how remote the place. But though witchcraft had been declared a crime by the Church in 1480 and had been prosecuted under civil (that is, non-religious) law for centuries previously, the time of the most widespread fear and persecution of Witches did not come until the seventeenth and eighteenth centuries in England and her colonies. There, partly because the conflict between Catholicism and Protestantism stimulated fanatics on both sides, there occurred periods of genuine hysteria when anyone might find himself accused of witchcraft on malicious or mistaken evidence. A great deal has been written about the cruelty and injustice of the Witch trials, particularly those in Scotland and in Salem, Massachusetts—so much, in fact, that the trials themselves probably helped end the persecutions by alerting the public to the abuses of justice that took place. Witchcraft is no longer a crime in any major European nation, and there is even a perfectly open organization of self-proclaimed Witches that asserts it has revived the more beneficial of the old magical practices—the rituals of fertility and health for all creatures.

And there the matter would rest if it were not for one thing. The picture we have painted so far shows a group of people engaged in a religious movement of a pagan and anti-Christian nature, which was shocking to conventional morality but which probably harmed no one but the participants. That is not really all.

The evidence from the Witch trials gives example after example of persons who claimed to have been injured by a Witch or Witches. Their cattle died, their houses burned, their children fell into trances or fits, they themselves became paralyzed, broke out with boils, or in some cases died from unknown causes. In the humane rush to show that the Witch trials were parodies of justice based on superstition and evidence obtained under torture, many writers have failed to point out that *witchcraft sometimes works.* In this book we have again and again come across the importance of belief—the idea that reality is what you think it is. Now that doctors have begun to make serious studies of the effects of the mind upon the body, there is no question that a person can suffer real illness (and perhaps in extreme cases even death) if he is sufficiently convinced that these misfortunes are inescapable. In a time when the power of Witches was universally believed in, at least among the less educated, some of the complaints about witchcraft were probably perfectly true. The process has recently been studied in certain tribes where the witchcraft of ill-wishing is still practiced with a fair amount of success, and there is no reason to suppose that it would not work as well anywhere, always assuming that *the victim believes in the power of the Witch*.

V

THE HALFWAY PEOPLE

And there be mongrel and ambiguous
shapes, between a human
and a brutish nature.

—Montaigne

UP TO THIS POINT the beings we have met have been basically human in appearance. With a few exceptions they have usually had two arms, two legs, one head, and the right number of other features to seem fairly familiar. In man's imagination, however, there was nothing to keep the Impossible People from having wings, claws, horns, hoofs, tails, fangs, scales, or snouts in bewildering variety. Nor was there any reason why mythological beings had to keep the same shape all the time, as man is forced to do. As a result, many are, so to speak, no more than half human. These Halfway People may be divided into two groups. Some are roughly half animal and half human all their lives, while others may look entirely human at one time and entirely animal at another.

Among the many part-animal beings in the mythologies of the world, it is interesting to note that some have always been more popular than others. For example, it may be that there are sheep-men some-where, but no one ever seems to have heard of them. Although the sheep is one of the most important domestic animals in many areas where the grazing is too sparse for cattle, this notoriously silly beast does not seem to have inspired anyone to wish to be like it. Apparently an animal must be powerful, dangerous, or otherwise remarkable in order to become the subject of this sort of legend.

Another domestic animal, the horse, has been much more popular among the creators of the Halfway People. Man's relationship with the horse has been a long and affectionate one, beginning thousands of years ago when the ancient hunters discovered a creature that was better to ride than to eat. From the mounted Mongol hordes and the magnifi-cent cavalry of the early North African kingdoms through the Spanish invaders of the New World, the men on horseback were the conquerors, bringing awe and terror to those who fought only on foot.

The Centaurs are among the best known of the Halfway People, with their great warhorse bodies out of which rise men's torsos, arms, and heads in place of horses' necks. Their name means "those who round up bulls" and some have suggested that when the southern Greeks first saw a tribe of mounted bull-herders in northern Thessaly, they thought the strangers were of one piece with their horses. Another view is that the actual Centaurs were a clan which worshipped a horse-god or totem and that their emblem was that of a man-horse. In either case, we know that the peoples of Central and South America did in fact make the mistake attributed to the early Greeks and believed (because horses were unknown in the New World at that time) that the Spanish ex-plorers and their horses were a single new breed of monster.

106

In the earliest tales the Centaurs were savage, gross, and cruel, confirming the idea that they were a tribe less civilized than the Greeks. Perhaps the Centaurs learned from their more peaceable neighbors, or perhaps the later tales show something of the Greek respect for the horse, since the Centaurs soon came to be thought of as both strong and noble. The Centaur Chiron was supposed to have been educated by the god Apollo and his sister Artemis and to have been in turn the teacher of many of the greatest heroes of Greek legend, among them Theseus and Jason. But though he was skilled in both soothsaying and medicine, Chiron was not able to cure himself from a wound he received at the hands of Herakles. Then, being unable to die because a Centaur was of course immortal, he remembered the fate of Prometheus, who had been sentenced by the gods to eternal torture because he had brought the gift of fire to man. Old and in pain, the Centaur prayed to Zeus to be allowed to trade his immortality for Prometheus' mortality. The god was roused to pity by such a noble request, and thus Chiron died while Prometheus joined the gods on Mount Olympus.

Some writers have seen a connection between the Centaurs and beings of the Indian Vedic tradition called Gandharvas. Like the Centaurs, the Gandharvas are man-horses possessed of divine wisdom. They are also the mates and pursuers of the Nymphs called Apsaras. Other sources say they play heavenly music and are the guardians of the sacred plant called Soma.

Not all of the men-horses are friendly to man. The British Isles are the home of several fabled horse-like beings ranging from mischievous to downright horrible. In Ireland, for example, one finds tales of the Pooka, who usually looks like a shaggy colt hung with chains.

The Halfway People

The Pooka spends most of his time frightening travelers in lonely places, but he is also said to do useful work just as if he were a Brownie.

The Grant is one of the few mythical beings who regularly appear in towns. He is the shape of a yearling colt, but he goes on his hind legs like a man and has fiery eyes. You may see the Grant at noon or just after sundown, when he runs through the streets pursued by barking dogs. His appearance is a warning of danger.

There is also the frightful Nuckelavee, a monster which comes up out of the sea in Scotland. Though the Nuckelavee looks like a huge horse and rider, he is really one animal. Furthermore, he has no skin and his breath is like a pestilence. His mouth is wider than that of even the biggest horse—a gaping split along his whole head, which one tale says is three feet across. The only escape from the Nuckelavee is to cross a stream or river because (like Demons, Devils, and other creatures of hell) the monster cannot cross running water.

About as popular as the horse among the Halfway People is the goat, whose contribution to the anatomy of Devils we have already noted. The Satyrs have the horns, tails, and hind legs of goats and walk upright like men. Their faces have the features of mischievous boys, and they love to dance and caper (the very word "caper" comes from the Latin word for goat). They are wood spirits who frequent groves and hillsides, and like the Indian Gandharvas they are wonderful musicians. The fact that Greek carvings usually show the Satyrs with low foreheads, snub noses, and wide mouths has lead some writers to guess that they may be derived from monkeys or apes. Certainly there is something not quite human about Satyrs' faces and like most beings they have their less charming side. The Satyrs are part of the following of Diony-

109

sus, the god of wine and pleasure. During the drunken revels of Diony-sus the Satyrs forget all decency and run through the woods in mad pursuit of any Nymph or mortal girl they happen to meet. The Satyrs have some rather rare cousins who have the hindparts of horses and are called Sileni.

Though we have already seen that there are links between the Satyrs and the Devils of later times, there is at least one story of a Satyr who tried to cast off paganism and enter the Christian church. Sir John De Mandeville was the fourteenth-century author of a book which proves him to have been either a great world traveler or a most accom-plished liar. In his account of his alleged travels, Mandeville includes a tale from the Middle East about a holy hermit who was approached by a Satyr begging the hermit to pray for him so that the Satyr's soul might be saved. To show the truth of his story, Mandeville said that he had seen the head of the Satyr in Alexandria, which seems to indicate that the hermit rather ungraciously killed the creature. (Mandeville, incidentally, calls the pagan being a Centaur but describes him as a Satyr, just to add to the confusion between goat- and horse-men.)

It is not impossible that the Satyrs' cousins the Fauns eventually became part of England's folklore. At least tales of those mischievous little beings with pointed ears and goat's horns who were companions of the god Faunus were surely brought there by the Romans in the days when their empire stretched as far as southern Scotland. The Fauns are very much like the Scottish Urisks, who are half human and half goat and sometimes help with such jobs as cattle herding. The rest of their time the Urisks spend in the wild hills or near waterfalls. However, they are said to get lonely for human company and sometimes give a fright to travelers who take them for less harmless beings. The Urisks have clan gatherings at certain times of the year, the favorite spot for which is said to be near Loch Katrine.

There is a sort of female version of the Urisk, called the Glaistig. Though she also is part goat, the Glaistig has a bewildering assortment of other habits usually associated with Faeries (misleading travelers, doing tasks paid for with milk) or Water Sprites (sitting in streams and asking to be carried across). An interesting detail is that a traveler is safe from her if only he won't tell her what kind of weapon he has— demonstrating once again the magical power of names.

In connection with the various hoofed animals, we should surely say a word about that famous monster, the Minotaur. Half human and half bull, though there is no agreement on which half was which, the Minotaur of myth lived on the island of Crete in the center of a maze so complex that one could wander in it for years. Those who were put into this maze, the Labyrinth, never came out, for when they eventually reached its center they were devoured by the Minotaur, who lived only on human flesh. The story of how the hero Theseus killed the Minotaur and found his way out again by following a thread that he had unwound behind him is too well known to need repeating in detail. What is unusual is that for once we have a fairly solid idea of the reality that hides in the center of the myth.

Excavations on Crete in the last century brought to light the palace of the Cretan sea kings, whose realm flourished well before the Greek mainland became the leading center of Mediterranean civilization. This palace was huge by any standards and was known as The House of the Double Axe—the "Labrys"—from which the name Labyrinth is derived. And we know, too, of a king who lived in this complex maze of rooms and corridors. He was not only the ruler of Crete, but the chief priest and actual embodiment of the Cretan bull-god. From documents and at least one ritual mask that has been found, we learn that the king was required to appear in the costume of the god on certain ceremonial occasions. And since he was reported by the Greeks, from whom we get the legend, to eat human flesh, is it not likely that the seven youths and seven maidens who were periodically sent as tribute from Athens to Crete were killed in the very beautiful but dangerous dance-games with live bulls which the paintings in the Labyrinth show us were held to honor the bull-god? For the victims of this ritual, danger did indeed lurk in the heart of the Labyrinth.

There are, of course, other interpretations of the Minotaur myth, and some of them may be equally true. The myth-makers were not bound by the modern notion that if an object or idea is one thing it cannot at the same time be another—that because we know that the Moon is a relatively barren satellite of the planet Earth, 2,160 miles in diameter, it cannot *also* be the changeable face of all women, the ball chased by the sun Dragon, or even the cookie that is constantly being eaten by the celestial pig. The loss is ours, not that of the poets who made the myths.

One of man's dearest wishes has always been to fly in the air—a dream which only recently became possible, with the invention of the ascension balloon, plane, glider, rocket belt, and, perhaps best of all, the parachute. Even now there is nothing that will let us imitate exactly the free glide, hover, and swoop of real birds, so possibly this longing for flight explains why there are so many different kinds of airborne beings in mythology. Of course the most obvious flying men are the gods of many religions who are almost always thought to live "up there somewhere." Next are the Angels and other winged protective spirits, as we have seen. In addition to those, Greek myths, among others, supply us with beings not so attractive. We must remember that the air is the home of the bat, the vulture, and the carrion crow, as well as that of the eagle and the lark.

Harpies are some of the nastiest beings in any mythology. Their bodies are those of birds of prey, their faces belong to evil crones, and for some curious reason they also have bear's ears. The Harpies lived together in a flock and were sometimes sent by the gods to punish individuals who had offended them. They were both greedy and filthy, and would swoop down on their victim while he was at table, gobbling everything edible and leaving behind only a foul mess. They sound, indeed, a little like particularly bold pigeons at an outdoor cafe. Wherever they went they spread stench and famine, though their names in Greek show they had once been nothing but storm goddesses. No one seems to know where they got their vile table manners.

The Sirens are a little more attractive than the Harpies, but no less dangerous. There is some confusion about their appearance, and medieval artists often gave them fish tails like Mermaids (who will be discussed in Chapter VI). The true Sirens of Greece, however, were shaped like beautiful women as far down as the navel, while the rest of their bodies was winged and feathered like a bird's. It was said that when a ship sailed by their rocky seacoast perches they would sing and cry out to the sailors with voices so sad and beautiful that many were dashed to death on the cliffs below, too enraptured even to notice that they were sailing to disaster. In some older versions of the story, the sailors were lulled to sleep, and the Sirens flew down and ate them.

The redoubtable Odysseus was one of the few ever to escape the lure of the Sirens. He ordered his men to stuff their ears with wax so that they could not hear the Sirens' song, while he made sure that he himself was tied firmly to the mast of the ship and so unable to give in to the desire to go nearer.

Some writers on mythology have explained the Sirens by saying they represent nightingales, birds that sing so beautifully they seem to have the range and tone of women's voices. Perhaps. But one would think the occasions when bird songs caused shipwrecks would be few. Another proposal is that the Sirens were originally conceived of as dead souls who were jealous of the living and wished to lure them to death. This idea is more plausible, since myths of many cultures say the souls of the dead have bird's wings and thirst for blood.

Among the Halfway People snakes must be nearly as popular as birds. In India the cobra was the inspiration for a whole mythical kingdom of beings called Nagas, who had human heads, or heads and torsos, joined to cobra's bodies. With their wives, the Naginis, the Nagas ruled an underground realm of glittering splendor. Since the cobra is one of the world's most impressive venomous snakes, it is not surprising that the Nagas were regarded with a mixture of awe and dread.

A similar kind of snake people is found all the way across the globe in the stories told by the Araucanians of Chile. Called the Cherruve these snake-people look very much like the Nagas. They are believed to be the cause of comets and shooting stars, which are omens of disaster in that part of the world.

In the mythology of Greece snakes figure in the features of a race of Giants, brothers of the Titans, whose legs are serpents with the heads where the Giants' feet ought to be. There are also the snake-haired Gorgons. These mythical creatures have grinning female faces, boar's tusks, golden wings, and bronze hands in addition to their writhing, hissing hairdos. In the original myth there were only three Gorgons and of the three only the one named Medusa was mortal. They lived together in the westernmost isles known to the Greeks, which were called the Hesperides. Anyone who had the misfortune to look at one of the Gorgons would immediately drop dead or be turned to stone—reports disagree. The hero Perseus was the only man to survive an encounter with the Gorgon. The myth says he managed to kill Medusa with a golden sickle while gazing in a mirror in order not to look directly at her deadly face.

Though there have been numerous and confusing efforts to unravel the meaning of the Gorgons, none has been entirely successful, perhaps because it is not certain exactly what part of the world the Greeks meant by the Hesperides. Were the Gorgons a group of Libyan snake priestesses or a tribe ruled by women in ancient Ireland? Once again, we must admit that we do not know.

It is rather a relief to turn to some beings described by the irrepressible thirteenth-century traveler Marco Polo. On his remarkable journey to China, Polo heard detailed accounts of a tribe he called the Dog-headed Men who lived in Madagascar. Through Polo's report and some others, the Dog-headed Men got into books of natural history, where they stayed until skeptics of later times threw them out on the grounds that they were obviously impossible. It is pleasant to be able to record that fairly recently a large species of lemur called the indris was found living quietly in Madagascar, where it had been all along. The indris looks much like a small man in outline, especially since, unlike most other lemurs, it does not have a long tail. However, it does have a decidedly doglike snout, and all in all one may say Marco Polo proved himself a fairly accurate reporter in this instance.

A very similar story can be told of the Tailed Men, who were widely believed in by Europeans during the period of world exploration. Of course, from earliest times conflicts between one group of people and another have taken the form of insults, and one of the commonest has been the notion that one's enemies have tails. (As recently as the last century it was whispered by their neighbors in the English county of Devon that all Cornishmen had tails.) The implication is that those who are thus equipped are not quite human and therefore do not deserve to be treated with any consideration—a particularly cruel and unfeeling idea. Belief in Tailed Men must have been strengthened when it was noticed that occasionally an otherwise normal baby is born with a few inches' worth of tail. Like certain other rare birth defects, this trait is a leftover from the remote period of human evolution when our pre-ape ancestors did indeed have tails. However, the fact that such babies were born must have confirmed the rumors about Tailed Men which became common in Europe after the fifteenth century. At that time voyagers to Africa, India, and the Far East began to bring back vivid accounts of areas where the whole population had tails. Many of these stories were highly exaggerated, claiming that the Tailed Men lived in villages, engaged in trade with other groups, and possessed language and culture. But in essence the reports were quite true; they merely reflected the European sailors' first encounters with the larger kinds of monkeys such as baboons, langurs, and macaques.

No one has yet found a similar grain of truth in the description of the Lamia, a very remarkable being who first appears in classical mythology as a simple woman-headed snake who was supposed to suck her victims' blood. That was ordinary enough, if not very lovable. But when we next meet the Lamia in the pages of the great Renaissance writers on natural history, she has been strangely transformed. Now she has the foreparts of a bear and the hindparts of a goat, to which are added the head and breasts of a woman and Dragon's scales. Just to increase the confusion, some writers chose to call her by the alternative name of Phairie, though anything less Faerylike is hard to imagine.

Another mythical being usually thought of as female is the Sphynx. The Great Sphynx of Egypt is among the most ancient and best-known compound creatures in the world, since the huge statue by that name has been astonishing tourists for five thousand years. Yet this particular Egyptian Sphynx is more properly referred to by its Greek name Harmakhis or the Egyptian Hor-m-akhet, meaning Horus-who-is-on-the-horizon, and is alone among the better known Sphynxes of legend in *not* being female. Instead, the Great Sphynx has the head of the Pharaoh Khephren attached to a lion's body. It is likely that the reason the Great Sphynx is commonly referred to as "she" is that the ceremonial wig of the Pharaoh led people of later times to think the statue had a woman's hair style.

117

Sixty feet high by one-hundred-eighty feet long, the Sphynx Harmakhis still guards the nearby tomb of the mortal man whose head it bears. The meaning of the Sphynx's vigil is apparent from its Egyptian name. Horus was the sun god and Horus-who-is-on-the-horizon is the rising sun, always a symbol of new life and resurrection. The Pharaoh himself (like the Cretan bull-king and many others) was supposed to represent the god to his people, so it was neither vanity nor blasphemy for Kephren to endow the statue with his own face. As for the lion's body, the lion was often a symbol of the sun, both because of the golden mane and because, in the desert climate of North Africa, the strength of the sun is as dangerous as that of a savage beast.

No one is quite sure how much direct connection there is between the Egyptian Sphynx and the obviously similar being found in the art and myths of Greece and the rest of the Near East. Still equipped with a lion's body, this other member of the species has wings in addition to its woman's head and breasts.

Like many other mythical beings, Sphynxes are fond of asking riddles. Yet riddles are never just a game in myths, or rather they are very important games in which the penalty for being counted out is death. The road to the Greek city of Thebes was the haunt of a Sphynx who preyed upon travelers until the coming of the hero Oedipus, who so angered her by answering her riddle correctly that she threw herself into the sea. The question that the Sphynx posed to Oedipus was this: What has four feet in the morning, two feet at midday, and three feet in the evening? "Man," answered the hero, discerning that a baby crawls on all fours, an adult stands upright, and an aged person walks with the aid of a stick.

119

The Greek Sphynxes may have been sun symbols like the Harmakhis, since the lion was frequently joined with the high-flying eagle for that purpose. Another suggestion is that the Sphynx was an ancient goddess whose lion-bird body showed that she had dominion over both earth and sky. The sixteenth-century naturalist Conrad Gesner even went so far as to say that the Sphynxes were confused versions of baboons, some of which do indeed have lion-like manes and tails with rather human faces, if not wings. Later writers, however, have felt that Gesner carried the quest for natural explanations too far.

Now we come to a group of beings who sound so bizarre that it is hard to know how to classify them. In Iroquois tales there appear characters called the Big Heads, a very appropriate name since that is precisely what they are. Shaped like enormous heads, they are covered with thick hair and their only limbs are two paws with sharp nails. They have flaming eyes and gaping mouths, and to anyone who thought he had seen them flying among the storm clouds supported only by their streaming hair they must have been a very fearsome sight. Like ordinary Giants with bodies, however, the Big Heads don't appear to be very bright. In one story a greedy Big Head saw an Iroquois girl eating roasted chestnuts from the fire and accidentally killed himself by swallowing, not the chestnuts, but the burning logs.

The ever-inventive Sir John De Mandeville supplied the folklore of Europe with some astonishing notions about the strange people who lived in distant places. From him came the account of a group of Ethiopians known as Monopods (from the Greek meaning "single-foot") for the very good reason that they were supposed to have only one leg in the middle of their bodies. The Monopods' single legs ended in very large, flattened feet, and Sir John reported that they got along very well in that shape and found the size of their feet a convenience in a hot climate, for they could use them as sunshades while lying on their backs. What, if any, reality could have underlain this remarkable fabrication, it is difficult to imagine. Though it may seem amusing to us now, it indicates how willingly people will believe the most absurd things of other people, if only they live far enough away. Mandeville also reported a tribe in the land of Ind (India) whose skins were supposed to be green and yellow. He said nothing further about the green-and-yellow men, however, except that the poor fellows lived beside a river that teemed with thirty-foot eels. In that case their green and yellow color might have been due to chronic fright.

Perhaps the oddest looking of all the Halfway People appeared in tales from the Isle of Man. He was Mannanan Mac Lir, and he combined his human features with those of an object, rather than an animal. Persons who claimed to have seen him reported that he was shaped like a spoked wheel with three running legs. Surprisingly, the weird appearance of Mannanan is quite simple to account for. Just such a three-legged wheel appears in carvings and pottery designs from the island's pre-Christian times, when it represented the sun in the form of a wheel, a very common symbol. The three-legged sun-wheel was not supposed to be a *picture* of Mannanan (the sun hero for whom the island is named), but was instead his personal sign or signature, like a potter's mark or cattle brand today. It was only in later times that the meaning of the running wheel was forgotten and the hero appeared in the people's imagination in a new and peculiar form.

If you are especially fond of horrors, you are sure to like the

Manticore, who is the author's personal choice for the title of Being Least Desirable to Meet on a Dark Night. (Second prize goes to the Nuckelavee.) The Manticore has a lion's body and a tail that ends in a poisonous sting, like the scorpion's. His head, however, is that of a man and his face is particularly blood-curdling. Beneath eyes of fiery red the Manticore's mouth extends almost from ear to ear, and each jaw displays three rows of pointed teeth, like a shark's. Perhaps the most horrible thing about the Manticore is that in his pictures the rest of his face looks so disarmingly like that of a rather nice gentleman with a well-kept beard and dashing moustaches. The teeth give him a hideous smile, and it comes as no surprise at all that the Manticore feeds on human beings. His name comes from a Persian word meaning man-eater, and he is said to frequent mountains and wild country, where he leaps upon passersby and devours them on the spot. He is famous for his jumping ability and one other curious detail is that he has a high, shrill voice that has been compared to the sound of flutes.

There have been many explanations proposed for the Manticore. Some say, apparently from a false interpretation of the name, that he is nothing more than the man-eating tiger of India and Persia. On the other hand, Samuel Johnson's great eighteenth-century dictionary defines the word "mantiger" as "a large monkey or baboon," and Dr. Johnson was not the last to propose such a connection. The reasoning behind this is much the same as that which suggested the baboon as an ancestor of the Sphynx. Although there are no baboons in Persia as it is today defined, the Persian empire at its height included some of the North African lands where baboons *are* found. And before we dismiss the idea altogether, it might be fair to recall that baboons certainly run

and leap with great agility, that they have shrill voices (shriller, anyway, than a tiger's) and that they can make very formidable opponents.
The adult males of many baboon species have been known to fight off
leopards, and their teeth are a match for those of the larger carnivores.
Lastly, it has been suggested that the Manticore is a man-tiger in a
second sense—that he is a human being who can change himself into a
tiger. This shape-shifting, as it is called, is a very old idea indeed, and is
the central characteristic of a whole group of the Halfway People to
whom we will now give our attention.

If one mentions the subject of men who change into animals, the
first example that usually comes to mind is the Werewolf. For centuries
this creature haunted the imaginations of people in all parts of Europe
and belief in him has probably not entirely died out to this day in the
eastern parts of the continent. It comes as a surprise to most of us,
however, to learn that there are many other kinds of were-beasts besides the wolf. (*Were*, by the way, is derived from an Anglo-Saxon
word meaning simply *man*, and is pronounced to rhyme with spear.)
Literally all around the world one may find tales involving shape-
shifting, and the central part in the story is usually played by the largest
carnivore of that particular region. Thus there are Were-leopards and
Were-hyenas in Africa, Were-jaguars in the Americas, Were-tigers in
India (whether or not they are Manticores), Were-foxes in China, and
Were-bears in the far north, as well as the common Werewolf. In general, the habits of all these beings are much alike, though we know more
of the horrid details of the life of the Werewolf because he has been so
thoroughly studied.

The Werewolf must take many of his characteristics from the

early European farmer's fear of the wolf. Those of us who have seen wolves in zoos sometimes regard them as big friendly dogs, and many animal lovers have declared them to make fine pets. This view was not shared by the inhabitants of Europe's wilder forest and mountain regions. To these people the wolf was a relentless enemy who slaughtered their flocks and whose ravenous appetite was only matched by his cunning. He was the embodiment of stealth and the thirst for blood, and the sound of his howling brought terror to those who sat within ill-lighted cottages on snowy nights.

The Werewolf in his animal form is a kind of super-wolf, bigger and hungrier than an ordinary wolf, and with a man's brain power to reinforce his wolfish instincts. Werewolves will eat anything that crosses their paths, but unlike true wolves they go out of their way to gorge themselves on human flesh. They are not at all afraid of fire or armed men and will leap through windows to get at their victims, sometimes terrorizing a whole town in a single night. Some Werewolves seem not to care about eating their prey, but only want to lap up its warm blood. As you might imagine, it takes a lot of blood to satisfy a full-grown Werewolf, and one can picture the carnage that was supposed to have occurred in the year 1542 when the city of Constantinople became as infested with Werewolves as a granary with rats. The plague was so terrible that the Emperor Suleiman II was forced to lead a regiment of cavalry against the Werewolves and one hundred fifty of them were killed, according to contemporary accounts. The hysteria must have resembled that of the later witch hunts.

The more usual thing is for Werewolves to appear one at a time, and one is quite enough. The most terrifying aspect of these monsters is that in their human form they may be anyone. Like Witchhood, with which it must not be confused, Werewolfery can occur in persons of any age, sex, or position, from the lowest to the highest.

There are two forms of Werewolfery, voluntary and involuntary. The first is less common and involves the subject's making a pact with the Devil. Wicked Magicians have been known to do this in order to further their evil designs. In such cases, the Werewolf concocts an ointment that produces the transformation when rubbed on the body.

However, the large majority of Werewolves are of the involuntary kind. That is, the wolfish appetite comes upon them against their will and is usually thought of as a kind of disease or possession by Demons. Then, no matter what respectable citizens they may be at other times, they must change to wolf form and give in to the terrible bloodlust that seizes them. The prescribed time for the change is at midnight by moonlight in some deserted spot. Often the Werewolf makes a magic circle on the ground and leaves his clothes in it, since he must be naked at the time of transformation. The purpose of the circle is to protect the clothing while the Werewolf is on his gruesome errand, for if someone finds and hides or destroys a Werewolf's clothes he will be unable to change back into human shape.

In times when Werewolves were, or were feared to be, all around, much attention was naturally given to the subject of how to identify one in his human form. Fortunately, the task became easier the longer the Werewolf lived, for Werewolfery grows progressively stronger in its hold upon its victim. Though at first he may show no outward signs of his nature, the Werewolf gradually becomes more and more completely dominated by his wolfish desires, as with someone in the later

stages of alcoholism or drug addiction. The Werewolf may then be known by his eyebrows, which often grow together in the middle. Pointed ears are also a suspicious sign, particularly if they grow more pointed as time goes on. The suspected Werewolf should be watched to see if he lopes stealthily when he thinks no one is watching him. Does the suspect have extra long fingernails and strong, sharp teeth (which in advanced cases may turn black or red)? Does he begin to shun daylight in favor of wandering about at night? Has he more than normal hair on his body, especially on the palms of the hands? Are his first and second fingers the same length? Do his eyes burn with a feverish light or glow red at night? Does he prefer raw meat to cooked or order his steaks extremely rare? Above all, does he have scratches or wounds on his body which he cannot account for? This last is the surest way to tell a Werewolf, for an injury he receives in his wolf form will also be visible on his human body.

Well then, once you have identified a Werewolf, what is to be done? The answer depends on who the monster is in ordinary life. If he (or she) is somebody's beloved husband or beautiful daughter, the relatives may insist on trying to cure him. Alas, those who try to provide therapy for Werewolves are often in for a losing battle. Exorcism by a priest, or preferably a saint, was often believed to be helpful, since it is agreed that the involuntary sort of Werewolf is possessed by a Demon. The cure rate from ceremonies designed to cast out Demons is low, however, and eventually the neighbors may demand that the Werewolf be executed for the good of the community. (There have been periods, too, when Werewolfery was considered a form of the crime of heresy and was legally punishable by death.) But destroying a Werewolf is not easy. Ordinary weapons are ineffective, though some say that a knife cut in the center of the forehead will either kill or cure. The only fairly reliable method is to fire at the Werewolf with a silver bullet, coin, or button.* It is even better if the silver bullet can be blessed by a priest just before firing, but priests are not always around at the right time. It is a comfort to everyone to know that once a Werewolf is dead, he will stay dead, and should not be confused with ghosts or Vampires in this respect. Less cheerful is the fact that several of those who wrote on the topic believed Werewolfery ran in families, so that there are certain districts which are plagued with recurring generations of the monsters. Or so the stories say.

When it comes to trying to unravel the origins of the Werewolf stories, the main problem seems to be too much evidence and too many theories. Almost every reference to wolves in the literature and history of the last three thousand years has been proposed as the origin of Werewolfery, from the story that the mother of the Greek god Apollo sometimes took the form of a wolf to the tradition that Romulus and Remus, the twin founders of Rome, were nursed by a she-wolf. All that is really proved by those references is that the wolf has played a part in myth and religion since very ancient times. But that, as we have just seen, is equally true of the horse, the goat, the lion, the bull, the snake, and a tremendous number of other beasts. Furthermore, we have already met the many-formed Slavic Polevik and Ovinnik, the deceptive

---

*The silver bullet is, in fact, a popular defense against any creature of the Devil and is equally useful against Vampires. They, by the way, do not belong among the Impossible People because they are not superhuman beings but merely The Dead, that is, they are ordinary human bodies that rise up from the grave.

Hag, and the many kinds of were-beasts which show that the Werewolf *kind* of transformation is worldwide and must have grown from many contributing sources.

First, there is always the exceptionally dangerous (but thoroughly real) individual animal—wolf, bear, tiger, hyena, jaguar, or whatever —whose strength and cunning make it seem almost immortal. Sometimes an animal which turns to man-killing (a rare thing, zoologists say, in spite of the tall tales) brings so much terror and destruction and is so hard to catch that it is natural to wonder whether the beast has intelligence beyond that normal for an animal. Or was he standing in the crowd in human form while the hunt was planned?

It is also true that there are or have been many groups of people who take a certain animal for their totem, a sort of combination guardian and ancestor. In such cases there are often ceremonies in which members of the group may dress and act like the totem animal in order to show their kinship. If the totem animal is a large and dangerous one strangers who witness the rituals may get the wrong idea about what is going on. That is especially true of cases in which the procedure included murder, as with the (long-outlawed) leopard societies of equatorial Africa, whose members tore their victims to death with iron claws in imitation of their patron the leopard.

By no means all examples of shape-shifting are so bloody. Also from Africa, this time from the Zambesi region, comes the tale of a young wife whose husband always seemed able to bring home a supply of milk, even in bad seasons when other men's herds ran short. The girl became curious (no one in a story of this type ever leaves well enough alone) and followed her husband when he went out one day, only to hear him sing a strange song and turn into a hyena. In that shape the man ran up to a pack of hyenas, where the females gladly gave him their milk. (The story doesn't say how he carried it.) Anyway, the wife went home and not only remembered the song but taught it to her sister. The next day the two women teasingly sang the song to the husband just as he was leaving the house: "Ndcra ndera ndera, hi ndera we./Ndera ndera ndera-a-a./ Ndera ndera ndera ndera woye,/Ndera ndera ndera." The rough meaning of this magical ditty is: "Early in the morning call/Hyena, Hyena!/ There, there they go,/There they go over the hill./Follow, follow, follow." It was a nice song, but it had unexpected results. The young husband changed instantly into a hyena, galloped out the door, and was never seen again.

Another harmless shape-shifter is the fabled Swan-maiden. As graceful and beautiful in human as she is in bird form, a Swan-maiden will sometimes shed her feathery swan dress by a lake when she goes to bathe. At that time a mortal man can make her his own by stealing the dress, for like the Werewolf in reverse, the Swan-maiden cannot change back to her animal shape without it.

Like Giants, Dwarfs, and (as we shall see) Mermaids, Swan-maidens are found all around the world, at least wherever there are swans. They appear not only among the myths of India and northern Europe but in those of the Tartars living near the White Sea in Russia and of the Siberian Samoyeds, among others.

Swan-maidens are perplexing because they have so many features usually associated with Water Nymphs and yet have the indisputable habit of turning into birds. The situation is only made more complicated by the obvious association of swans with water. Were the Swan-

maidens once emblems of the white clouds that float in the blue sky as swans float on the blue water, clouds that sometimes seem to come down to the water themselves in the form of reflections? It is very hard to say. The problem is probably best shown in myths about the Apsaras of India. They are described as beautiful maidens who haunt springs and wells and are beloved by the music-loving Gandharvas, the horse-men mentioned earlier. So far the Apsaras sound precisely like the Water Nymphs of Greek mythology, who were pursued through the woods by the Satyrs. In one typical story of an Apsara, however, the beautiful Urvasi runs away from her mortal husband because he has broken his vow never to let her see him naked. The abandoned husband, Pururavas, at last finds Urvasi swimming among a flock of swans on a lake. "What have I to say to you? I left you like the first dawn. Return home, Pururavas. I am like the wind and hard to capture," she says to him. However, she later relents and instructs him how to become one of the Gandharvas so that he may enjoy her love forever.

Plainly, the Swan-maidens, Werewolves, and other shape-shifters are all part of a folk tradition that is worldwide. Why, then, did the Werewolf have such a strong and enduring grip on the minds of the people of Europe? No doubt part of the reason lies in the climate of morbid superstition that sometimes prevailed in remoter areas. But medical research has recently come up with some very interesting speculations about Werewolfery as an actual disease or combination of diseases. It appears there are some relatively rare but genuine conditions that could have contributed a great deal to belief in Werewolves.

One of these conditions is hereditary hypertrichosis, a trait that, while otherwise harmless, results in the growth of fine silky hair all over the person's skin. It is recorded that a man named Peter Gonzales (born in the Canary Islands in 1556) displayed hypertrichosis and became, because of his oddity, a member of the court of Henry II of France. Gonzales passed on the characteristic to at least three of his children and presumably there have been other families from time to time who might have helped the Werewolf legend in this way.

There is also a disease named porphyria in which a group of pigments called porphyrins become present in the blood and elsewhere in the body. Porphyria is a truly horrifying illness, of which the precise cause and treatment are still not known. In it toxic substances combine to attack many parts of the body at once, sometimes producing insanity when the brain and nervous system are affected. Symptoms may include sensitivity to light, brought about by changes in the skin, sunken and unsteady eyes, and the presence of open sores not accounted for by physical injuries. Hairiness of the skin may also appear, and the teeth may even become red from pigment deposits. As damage to the brain progresses, the patient may behave very wildly and sometimes insist on wandering about at night, either to hide the unattractive symptoms of the disease or because of his increased sensitivity to bright light. It is not known that persons with porphyria crave human blood, but the other features of the description fit so well that it would be hard not to conclude that cases of the disease must have added fuel to the flame of the Werewolf terror. One need only add that a tendency to porphyria may, in some cases, be inherited, so that in that respect, too, it fits in with beliefs about Werewolves.

Finally, there are various kinds of strictly mental diseases in which the patient may come to believe himself to be a wolf or other animal.

Insanity of this sort might be inspired by the Werewolf legend itself, or might come about if the patient saw in himself some of the frightening symptoms of hypertrichosis or porphyria. Perhaps the early writers on the subject were correct in saying that some Werewolves were the victims, not of Demonic possession, but of a mental disease which they called lycanthropy—the *delusion* of being a Werewolf though of course both forms were thought to be the work of the Devil. In point of fact, those who suffered from lycanthropy or porphyria were scarcely better off than the suspected Werewolf in those days when beating and starvation were the routine treatments for mental illness. Like all the Halfway People in the last analysis, the Werewolf had his truest origin in the animal nature that man found within himself.

VI
THE PEOPLE OF THE SEA

I have heard the mermaids singing,
each to each;
I do not think that they will
sing to me.

—T. S. Eliot

OCEANS, SEAS, LAKES, rivers, streams, swamps, springs, cascades, torrents, brooks, ponds, puddles, pools: we have a great many names for the bodies of water that cover more than seventy percent of the earth's surface. *Our* bodies also are largely composed of water, and man has always been deeply fascinated with this substance that is so common, yet so necessary for his survival. The poet Carl Sandburg once called man "a sea animal living on land, wanting to fly the air." He was correct scientifically, as well as poetically, for of course the first ancestors of man and all land creatures did crawl up out of the sea, hundreds of millions of years ago. And if, as we have already seen, Sandburg's "animal living on land" peopled the air with Angels, gods, and Swan-maidens, he also expressed a certain homesickness, perhaps,

135

by filling the seas and rivers with imaginary beings something like himself.

In every part of the world there are beliefs about beings who live in water, and often these beings show a surprising family resemblance. By the time of the ancient Greeks tales about the two principal types of water-dwellers were already well established. The first type was the Nymphs, lovely young girls who mainly inhabited fresh water. Each spring or pond or river had its own Nymph, and water was their original home, although in later times groups of Nymphs moved into the forests and became the Oreads, Dryads, and Hamadryads mentioned in Chapter IV. Nymphs are beloved of both gods and men, and there are hundreds of stories about their romances, so many that the very word "nymph" in everyday language has come to mean a lovely and desirable girl.

But though these water women were dazzlingly beautiful, their love was not without dangers for mortal men. Teutonic mythology told of a being called the Nix (feminine, Nixe). The Nixies were most often young women who sat on river banks combing their long golden hair. Their singing was as enchanting as their faces, but a young man who embraced a Nixe would be dragged down to the bottom of the river and drowned. The Nix men also enticed mortals to their doom, though perhaps the maidens who loved them were near-sighted, for the Nix men had green teeth. The best protection against the enchantments of the Nixies was to keep a knife or nail in the bottom of your boat. In that belief we again recognize the power of iron to ward off the magical beings of pre-Christian times.

Apparently, however, there was no undying hostility between the

Nixies and the Church. In one folktale a priest who was walking along a riverbank one day was surprised to be confronted by a Nixe, who begged him most humbly for a blessing. Horrified at such a pagan apparition, the priest struck the ground with his staff and declared that sooner would the dead wood blossom than would a Nixe be saved. And immediately, says the story, the old man's staff burst into a shower of pink and white flowers, and the Nixe dived joyfully back into the river.

Different from the Nixe, though also Teutonic, was the Lorelei, a particular Water Nymph with habits like those of the Sirens. The Lorelei sat on a high cliff above the Rhine River, combing her hair with a golden comb and singing a song of haunting beauty and sorrow. Many sailors forgot themselves in the sound of her singing and were killed on the wicked rocks below.

Sometimes the relations of human beings and water women end tragically for the Nymph. In the Karanga language of Africa there is the story of a young man who won the love of a water sprite and persuaded her to come with him to the home of his family so they could be married. Before leaving the river the girl begged him not to let her become dry on the journey. However, the young man was so impatient to show off his lovely bride that he forgot to carry water with him. As they went farther and farther from her river home, she wilted and faded like a plucked flower until at last she died, despite her lover's heartbroken pleas.

One may wonder why most water spirits are female. The probable answer is that water has always seemed to have a special association with women, because women's bodies undergo changes over a twenty-eight-day period which appear to coincide with the phases of the moon.

138

The People of the Sea

Since the moon also controls the tides, it is easy to see why even the earliest men felt there must be some special link between women and water. It is not certain what, if any, is the actual connection of the moon with this particular human biological characteristic, but such cycles occur in many other places in nature as well. The linking of women to the changes of the moon and the tides is an extremely common one in mythology, even in cultures where the moon is thought of as masculine. Another important factor is the so-called waters of birth, the amniotic fluids that surround the baby with an artificial sea when it is in its mother's womb. The birth of every human being, and in fact of every mammal, is accompanied by the outflowing of these fluids. And since there is no more wonderful event than the birth of a new life, every fact surrounding birth had the greatest significance for the first men, the myth-makers who saw in this phenomenon further evidence that women were creatures of water.

So far, the water people we have discussed have looked almost entirely like human beings, although a little more beautiful than most. But special environments tend to influence those who live in them, so that just as Trolls came to look like mountains, water spirits often resemble fish or other water creatures.

Sometimes water people only show their fishy side at certain times or seasons. A legend from early medieval France tells of the noble knight Raymond de Lusignan, who one day met a most beautiful girl by a spring in the forest. Melusina was her name, and she agreed to marry Raymond on condition that he would never try to see her on Saturdays. But conditions like that are made to be broken and finally

Raymond was overcome by curiosity. He hid in his wife's bedroom one Saturday, only to discover to his horror that on that day his lovely Melusina had the tail of a fish. Afterward, though he tried to hide the fact that he had found out her secret, Raymond one day let slip his knowledge. Thereupon Melusina gave a dreadful cry and disappeared through the window, pausing only to say that she would thereafter hover over the castle whenever a new lord was about to be born. The fact that Melusina acted like a bird while looking like a fish reflects the confusion that existed in those days about Sirens. As we said in the last chapter, the original Sirens were singing bird-women. However, they later began to appear in the medieval bestiaries with both fish tales and wings, probably because their habit of luring sailors to their deaths was seen to resemble that of the Lorelei and certain kinds of Mermaids. As for Melusina, she became the reputed ancestress of many noble families, including the Plantagenet kings of England.

Probably the earliest true fish-man was the Babylonian god Oannes, who first appeared about 5000 or 4000 B.C. (it is hard to place the date more accurately than that). Carved portraits of Oannes show him as a mature man with the squarish beard and tall headdress of the period. He swims with the human half of his body upright in the water, so that his scaly fish tail is at right angles to it. He was supposed to spend his days on land in human shape, returning to the sea at night. This habit indicates that Oannes may have begun as a god of the sun, which in most Mediterranean lands does indeed appear to sink into the western sea every evening. Oannes, therefore, must have been given his fish tail as a symbol of the daily east-west passage of the sun. Many other fish-tailed gods of ancient times probably shared this origin, though they later came to be thought of solely as gods of the sea. Oannes was also revered as a giver of knowledge and prophesier of the future, traits which later crop up again in Mermaids.

Among the Greeks we find few true Mermaids, but there were both the tailless Water Nymphs and the sea-going Tritons. Sons of the sea god Poseidon, the Tritons were rather terrifying to look at. They had scaly bodies, sharp teeth, and clawed hands. Unlike many water folk they were not particularly musical, but they did enjoy making a tremendous racket by blowing on conch shells. All in all, the Tritons seem to have embodied the stormier aspects of the sea, and they are thought to have been taken over by the Greeks from certain gods of Libya.

Elsewhere in Africa, in Nigeria, there was a powerful water god by the name of Olokun. He was almost a double Merman, for he had two large mudfish for legs, with the heads where his feet should have been. Olokun was believed to rule beneath the sea in a kingdom of incredible wealth and beauty, bright with pearls and coral.

Later times seem to have seen a multiplication of rather than a decline in the Merfolk. They have many names, like the Faeries, but seem closely enough related to be considered under one heading. The Dracs, for example, are water people said to live in the rivers of France and England. Because they are not able to nurse their own children, the Dracs have the habit of appearing on the surface of the water in the form of floating golden rings or wooden dishes. When a mortal woman sees one of these objects and reaches to fish it out of the water, the Drac returns to its true form and pulls her down beneath the river to care for its children.

Less pleasant even than the Dracs were the Vodyanoi of Slavic tradition. They lived in fresh water and could appear in any of several different shapes. Sometimes they looked like human beings with paws, horns, and tails, sometimes like huge men covered with grass and moss, red-eyed, and with noses as long as a fisherman's boot. Again, they might be old men with green hair and beards, or naked women combing the water from their long tresses. They might even be enormous, moss-grown fish or tree trunks with little wings flying over the water. Whatever form they had, the Vodyanoi grew older and younger with the phases of the moon and their beards (when they were in semi-human form and had beards) became white when the Moon was waning. They were generally enemies of human beings, and those whom the Vodyanoi succeeded in drowning became slaves in their underwater palaces, which were made of crystal and ornamented with gold and silver stolen from sunken ships.

In the highland legends of Scotland are found the Fuaths, who also delighted in drowning unwary mortals. They had yellow hair and webbed feet, as well as tails, horses' manes, and no noses. Plainly, they took some of their characteristics from the Faeries, for the Fuaths wore green and hated iron. However, the stories add that they cannot cross running water, which is very unusual for any of the water folk and may lead us to suspect that they have sold themselves to the Devil for some ill reason.

In northern Scotland, Ireland, and Scandinavia are to be found some People of the Sea who have the features of seals rather than of fish. They are called the Selchies or Roane, and the stories describe them as shape-shifters like those of the last chapter.

The People of the Sea

I am a man upon the land,
I am a Selchie in the sea,
And when I'm far frae every strand
My dwellin' is in Sule Skerie.

Thus speaks the Selchie himself in an old ballad of the Orkney Islands, from which the rock called Sule Skerry lies about fifty miles southwest in the Atlantic. The Selchies, like the seals themselves, need air to live, and their deep-water homes are caverns under the waves, in which they may also cast their skins and take human form. They have some very close relatives in the Shetland Islands. There the Sea-trows come ashore in the form of various animals with fish tails and also cast their skins in order to wander about on land.

There is little doubt that the numerous tales of the Selchies are the result of the long association of men and seals as hunters and hunted. For centuries seal fur, seal hide, seal meat, and seal blubber were essential to the people of those cold and sea-beaten coasts, both for daily survival and for profit. And as sometimes happens the same men who killed the seals grew to admire and love the animals which supported them and which were so very human in some ways. No one could fail to be moved by the seals' evident concern for their young, the fun-loving way they play in the waves, or the soft and rather sad expression in their big dark eyes. To the extent that men saw themselves in their prey, they were ashamed of killing, which must sometimes have seemed more like making war upon the helpless than it did like hunting. And so we find the Selchies, who share some traits with Mermaids but are really quite different.

143

It is not clear from the tales whether Selchies are all seals or some individual seals, or even whether they may not be a particular species of seal such as the large and beautiful gray seal. Some say that the Selchies were once human, the children of the legendary King of Lochlann, and that on them a spell was put so that "their sea-longing shall be land-longing and their land-longing shall be sea-longing" forever.

Whichever way it may be, the Selchies are strange folk to deal with, as a man named Angus Ruadh of Scotland was only one of many to learn. It seems this Angus Ruadh was a famous seal killer in his time, and one night he was awakened by a knock on the door of his hut. Angus got up and went outside, where he found a stranger who asked him if his name were Angus Ruadh, the seal killer. When Angus said it was that, the stranger told him he must come with him quickly to see a man who wished to arrange for the purchase of one hundred sealskins, a great lot of skins for one man to buy and very good business for Angus. Only, the stranger said, the deal had to be completed that very night. Then he took Angus up behind him on his horse and rode with him through the windy dark until they found themselves at the top of a sea cliff. The stranger hardly gave Angus time to look round, but pulled him down from the horse, clasped him in his arms, breathed a deep breath into his mouth, and jumped with him into the sea. Down they went in the cold blackness, only stopping on the sea floor, where they saw a door. The stranger opened the door and took Angus into a big room full of people who were crying and wailing as if to mourn the dead.

Poor Angus was frightened and bewildered beyond words, though some of the people spoke kindly to him, for all he could think was that he would never get back safe to his own home and family. Then the

144

stranger reappeared before Angus with a long knife in his hand. "Have you ever seen this knife before?" he asked. Shaking, Angus could only answer truly that he had indeed seen it, since it was his own knife that he had that day stuck into a seal which had swum off with it before being killed. "That seal was my father," said the stranger then, and to Angus' amazement he led him into another room, where lay an old seal with a great wound in his side. Those who were in the room explained to Angus that the wound could only be cured by the one who had made it, and when Angus put out his hand and closed the cut the old one jumped up in perfect health. After that, the Selchies asked Angus to swear that he would never kill or maim another seal. He did so gladly, for his eyes had been opened by what he saw. Then the same one who had brought him down took him up through the cold sea to the cliff top and then back to his cottage on horseback. Angus parted friends with the Selchie, who gave him his knife back, as well as a bag of Danish gold and an apology for the trick he had played on him. You may be sure, too, that from that day to the end of his life Angus Ruadh never harmed another seal.

The Merfolk in Irish legends are called Merrows, and like the Selchies they live on dry land under the sea. The Merrow women are very beautiful and perform great enchantments with the aid of the magical red caps they wear. The Merrow men, however, have long red noses, short finlike arms, and green teeth and hair. Merrows are unreliable and dangerous. Many human beings have been drowned through their spells.

Even stranger are the Blue Men of the Minch, the narrow piece of sea that divides the Outer Hebrides from western Scotland. They are a particularly treacherous kind of Merman, blue all over, who come swimming out to wreck passing ships. Like the Sphynx, they are fond of riddles, and a captain who is quick with his tongue may sometimes talk his way out of danger. The Blue Men are especially impressed with those who can speak in rhyme. Oddly enough, the Blue Men have a probable basis in history. They seem originally to have been so-called Blue Moors (actually Berbers), some of whom were captured and pressed into service by the Norse pirates who once preyed on shipping in the Hebrides. The men of this North African Berber tribe not only wore blue robes and veils over their faces, but, it has been suggested, took on the color of their clothing after a lifetime of contact with its blue dye. Whatever the truth of this last notion, the memory of dangerous blue-clad pirates still haunts the islands.

Of course the most famous of all the People of the Sea is the Mermaid. She is so firmly founded in folklore around the world that it was only in the last century that Mermaids were finally admitted to belong to legend rather than to natural history.

Like the sea itself, Mermaids are endlessly fascinating. They are most often said to be seen on calm, sunny days, when they either swim gracefully about the prow of your ship, their long tails flashing green and silver in the sun, or come up onto sea-washed rocks to comb their hair. In northern countries Mermaids are often blonde like the rest of the population, but they may have any sort of coloring at all. The Shawano Indians of North America say their ancestors were guided there from Siberia across the Great Salt Lake (the ocean) by a Merman who had green hair and the face of a porpoise, as well as two tails. With

the exception of this porpoise-faced variety, however, Merfolk are almost always beautiful.

Combing their hair is such a popular activity with Mermaids that in the medieval period they were hardly ever shown without a comb in one hand and a mirror in the other. Some writers have tried to explain this passion for hair-combing by saying that the sources of the medieval idea are ancient carvings showing Mermaids holding the lyre and the toothed plectrum with which it was played. Such an interpretation fits well with the traditional association of the water people with music and singing, and it is certainly true that the lyre and plectrum could be mistaken for a comb and mirror in some of the early portraits of Mermaids. Others suggest that the mirror was originally a disc representing the moon, showing yet again the mythological connection of the moon and the sea.

In the British Isles, where tales of Mermaids are very common, it is known that the best moment to capture one of the sea women is when she is combing her hair, for in order to do so she must remove the red cap she wears. Then, if a mortal can seize the cap, the Mermaid will be his as long as she cannot find the place where he has hidden it. This notion is much like the one about the clothes of the Swan-maiden and the Werewolf and points to another general rule of magic: you are what you wear.

Possession of a Mermaid's cap will certainly get you a more pleasant companion than a Werewolf, however. Mermaids have sometimes made happy marriages with mortals, and there are several families which claim to have a Mermaid in their ancestry. A Mermaid's descendants often inherit her gift of prophecy.

Sometimes the love affair is said to begin on the Mermaid's side.

Being famous for their singing, they are especially likely to fall in love with those who are skilled in music. In Cornwall, England, folk tell the tale of young Mathey Trewhella, who sang so beautifully that a local Mermaid used to come up to hear him. Eventually the sea woman lured the young man into the water and all his relations mourned him for dead. But many years later the captain of a ship anchored in Zennor harbor was approached by a Mermaid who asked him most politely to move his anchor. The great iron thing was blocking the door of her home, she explained, and until it was moved she couldn't return to her children and her loving husband Mathey Trewhella. To this day, one can go into the little fifteenth-century church of Zennor and see the Mermaid carved on a pew in memory of the event.

Mermaids may be beautiful, but to see one is more often than not an omen of storms or bad luck. They like to play catch among themselves with fish, and it is especially unlucky if the Mermaids throw fish toward your boat in the course of their game. To ward off disaster, some say one should throw something *toward* the Mermaid, preferably something made of iron, but that the last one to throw before the Mermaid disappears will soon be drowned.

It is even more dangerous to annoy a Mermaid than simply to see one. Padstow harbor in Cornwall is supposed to have filled up with silt because one of the townsmen had the bad judgment to shoot at a Mermaid, and the mists that put the Isle of Man out of touch with the mainland are also said to result from a Mermaid's displeasure. In another old tale a large stone on the coast of Scotland that had for years been known as the Mermaid's Seat was tipped into the sea by a local man, at which moment a Mermaid rose up out of the water and cursed his family with barrenness, saying, "Ye may think on your cradle, I'll

think on my stane [stone]/And there'll never be an heir to Lockdolian again."

Through many Mermaid stories runs a rather wistful feeling. Mermen seldom appear unless to woo the love of mortal maidens, and both Mermaids and Mermen seem to have an inextinguishable wish for something that can never be theirs. Many stories of the medieval period indicate that what they yearn for is a human soul. Ordinarily the Merfolk are thought of as mortal but not human. That is, though they are very long lived, they do die at last, and then they perish utterly because they have no souls. And in spite of the fact that Mermaids were often used by medieval preachers as examples of the false attractions of sin, it is plain that some of the Merfolk at least were able to make their peace with the Christian Church. A story of the first century A.D. relates that there was once an Irish girl named Liban (her name indicates that she was linked to a pagan goddess of that name) who was caught in a flood with her dog. Strangely enough they were not drowned but lived on under water. However Liban was unhappy in her watery life and wished that she could become a fish. In heaven God heard her wish and compassionately changed Liban into a Mermaid and her dog into an otter. For three hundred years she and her pet lived in this way until one day a missionary named Beoc heard her singing the story of her experiences. Beoc spoke to the strange pagan being and at last convinced her to come out of the sea and be received into the Church. A great crowd of saints gathered on shore to witness the miracle—so many, in fact that they fell to quarreling over which should take credit for the Mermaid's conversion. Nothing could dim Liban's joy at being redeemed from her soulless state, however. The tale says she left the sea without a backward glance and was granted the further blessing of going to heaven immediately.

Mermaids appear to play a large part in the history of the early Christianization of Ireland and Scotland. To this day round pebbles on the beaches of Iona are called Mermaid's tears. Perhaps the tears were shed by a gaggle of old women whom Saint Patrick is supposed to have turned into Mermaids in punishment for their refusal to be converted.

One of the reasons why belief in Mermaids was so persistent was that the sea still holds many mysteries for mankind. There are surely numerous species of living things in the world's oceans that are as yet unknown to science. Conspicuous land-dwellers like Giants might begin to seem unlikely as centuries went on, but who could say what was in the vast waters "out there"?

Another factor was that Mermaids had been vouched for by no less an authority than the Roman writer Pliny, who is often called the Father of Natural History. In the seventeenth-century translation of his works by Philemon Holland, Pliny says of Mermaids:

> It is no fabulous tale that goes of them; for . . . their bodie is rough and skaled all over even in those parts wherein they resemble a woman. For such a Meremaid was seen and beheld plainely upon a coast and neere to the shore: and the inhabitants dwelling neere, heard it afar off, when it was dying, to make a pitteous mone, crying and chattering very heavily.

One reason why this account was so convincing is perhaps that it doesn't sound at all like the romantic and beautiful singing Mermaid of the popular tales. Further, the authority of classical authors such as Pliny was so great that for centuries no one questioned that Mermaids were as real as whales, though most people had never seen either. During the medieval period it was believed that not only human beings but all land creatures had their counterparts in the sea. That theory is reflected still in the names of such animals as the sea lion, sea elephant, sea cow, sea horse, and sea anemone. There were even thought to be sea Centaurs and sea Unicorns, which would have been mythical twice over.

In addition, sober and otherwise reliable persons kept reporting Mermaids until long after the days when any educated man who claimed to have seen a Troll or a troupe of Dwarfs carrying picks and shovels, for instance, would have been laughed into silence. By the sixteenth century some skeptics such as the sharp-witted Sir Thomas Browne had already decided that Mermaids did not belong in books of natural history. However, in the year 1560, seven strange creatures were netted off the coast of Ceylon in the presence of several Jesuit priests and the physician to the Viceroy of Goa. All were willing to swear that the creatures were genuine Merfolk. In 1577 a Mermaid appeared near Samsoe in Denmark and, it was claimed, not only spoke to a peasant there, but correctly prophesied the birth of King Christian IV. The man who saw her said she was very beautiful although she admitted to being eighty years old.

Mermaid sightings began to come from the New World as soon as it was reached by explorers. On June 15, 1608, two men from the crew of Hendrik Hudson reported seeing a Mermaid.

This morning one of our companie looking overboord saw a Mermaid, and calling up some of the companie to see her, one more came up, and by that time shee was come close to the ship's side, looking earnestly on

153

the men: a little after, the sea came and overturned her: From the Navill upward, her backe and breasts were like a woman's (as they say that saw her) her body as big as one of us; her skin very white; and long haire hanging down behinde, of colour blacke; in her going down they saw her tayle, which was like the tayle of a Porposse and speckled like a Macrell. Their names that saw her were Thomas Hilles and Robert Raynar.

The controversy over Mermaids continued into the eighteenth century and in 1723 the Danish government established a Royal Commission to consider the matter. The Commissioners reported they had themselves encountered a Merman off the Faroe Islands. It roared at them and dived away, but not before they could see it well enough to record that it had deepset eyes and a black beard which "looked as if it had been cut."

By the beginning of the nineteenth century, many scholars had begun to deny the existence of Mermaids, but belief among the general public was still strong enough to support the owners of several "stuffed Mermaids" which were put up for commercial exhibit. A particularly famous example was on view in London's Egyptian Hall in the 1830's, and another formed part of the sideshow run by the incomparable P.T. Barnum.

The realities behind the Mermaid's alleged appearances were much less romantic than the legends. Most probably the ideas of the ancient sea gods and Water Nymphs were supported by accounts of various real animals.

The best candidate for a live Mermaid belongs to a family of sea-going mammals appropriately named sirenia, after the Sirens. They are

the dugong of the East Indies and the manatee of the Atlantic shores of Africa and South America. These animals, though they look somewhat like seals to the untrained eye, are in fact distantly related to the elephants, a fact which by itself makes them unusual enough. The manatee and the dugong are about the general size and bulk of a human being, or a little larger with two large flippers in front but no rear limbs, only a flattened, paddlelike tail. Both species have the habit of raising themselves half out of the water to survey the landscape or nurse their young, and there is no doubt that when they do this they resemble the traditional picture of Mermaids in general outline. Since they live only in tropical waters, the two species were of course largely unfamiliar to European explorers, and they must have accounted for at least a fair number of alleged Mermaids. In this connection one thinks particularly of the Mermen whose capture was witnessed by the Jesuits near Ceylon, an area once well stocked with dugongs.

It is too bad that a closer look at the manatee and the dugong shows them to be so very worthy of the other name by which each is known, which is sea cow. They are portly beasts with wrinkled, nearly hairless hides, and they have almost no necks and certainly no long floating tresses. Besides all that they have divided upper lips like those of camels, and they are not even very graceful swimmers. It must be a tribute to the power of man's imagination and the lonely life of the sailor that the placid and leathery sea cow could ever have taken shape in his mind as a Mermaid. But after all, Mermaids are famous for their enchantments.

Another animal that must have played a part in the Mermaid legend is the seal. We have already seen the role of this appealing creature in the stories of the Selchies. Surely seals occasionally seemed like

156

true Mermaids as well, especially as they can make a variety of uncanny noises which could well be compared to the "pitteous mone" of Pliny's specimen. Indeed those who live near the seals' breeding grounds in the islands off northern Scotland assert that seals can sing, though if that is so their songs must be older and lonelier than any known to human beings.

It should also be noted that web-fingered beings like the Fuath and some Mermaids may have been derived from the fact that webbed fingers and toes do sometimes appear in human beings, though rarely. Nowadays a simple operation can remove the webs, but in times past such individuals must often have been suspected of being Merfolk or descendants of Merfolk.

Also the mere fact of being able to travel in boats has sometimes been a source of wonder and confusion to peoples who are unfamiliar with seafaring. The Jicarilla Apache of the American southwest say (appropriately enough) that the white men were created by a god who took a walk to the eastward and found two blue-eyed fish. Similarly, the horse-herding Mongols of the plains of central Asia believed that the English were a tribe of amphibious beings like frogs when the two groups first came into contact in the 1840's. Legends have been made from beginnings even less substantial.

Then what about those stuffed Mermaids, some of which were very convincing to look at? Unfortunately it turns out that the manufacture of such curiosities was a small industry in Japan at one time. Japan also had a strong traditional belief in Mermaids, and some Japanese fisherman discovered that fish and monkeys, cleverly and carefully sewn together, could be sold to collectors for very nice prices.

At least a few fake Mermaids were *not* stuffed. July of the year

1825 was enlivened for the inhabitants of Bude, Cornwall, by the appearance of a highly visible and vocal Mermaid for several evenings running. The lady not only sat on a harbor rock in full view of everyone, but provided entertainment by singing "God Save the King" with patriotic vigor. We may share the probable disappointment of the people of Bude when it was revealed that the "Mermaid" was in fact Robert S. Hawker, who was the vicar (and apparently a humorous one) of the nearby town of Morwenstow. Hawker had equipped himself with a seaweed wig and wrapped oilskins around his legs for his performances. It seems the people of Bude were no different from the rest of us in seeing only what they want or expect to see.

In the end, then, the Merfolk are truly Impossible People, made from gods of former times, mistaken reports of real animals, misinterpretations of ancient artwork, natural oddities, hoaxes, and at least a dash of the permanent mysteriousness of the sea.

BIBLIOGRAPHY

Adams, W.H. Davenport, *Witch, Warlock, and Magician.* New York: J.W. Bouton, 1889.

Ausubel, Nathan, ed., *A Treasury of Jewish Folklore.* New York: Crown Publishers, 1948.

Aylesworth, Thomas G., *Servants of the Devil.* Reading, Mass.: Addison-Wesley, 1970.

Baring-Gould, Sabine, *Curious Myths of the Middle Ages.* New Hyde Park, N.Y.: University Books, 1967.

Benwell, Gwen, and Waugh, Arthur, *Sea Enchantress.* New York: Citadel Press, 1961.

Bodin, Walter, and Burnet, Hershey, *It's a Small World.* New York: Coward-McCann, 1934.

Botkin, B.A., ed., *A Treasury of New England Folklore.* New York: Crown Publishers, 1947.

Briggs, K.M., *The Anatomy of Puck.* London: Routledge & Kegan Paul, 1959.

——, *The Fairies in English Tradition and Literature.* Chicago: University of Chicago Press, 1967.

——, and Tongue, Ruth, eds., *Folktales of England.* Chicago: University of Chicago Press, 1965.

Burland, Cottie, *North American Indian Mythology.* Feltham, England: Paul Hamlyn, 1968.

Campbell, Joseph, *The Masks of God.* New York: The Viking Press, 1959, 4 vols.

Cannon, Dr. Walter B., "Voodoo Death." *American Anthropologist,* new ser. vol. 44, 2 (April-June, 1942) pp. 169-181.

159

Carrington, Richard, *Mermaids and Mastodons*. New York: Rinehart & Co., 1957.

Christie, Anthony, *Chinese Mythology*. Feltham, England: Paul Hamlyn, 1968.

Evans-Wentz, Walter Yeeling, *The Fairy Faith in Celtic Countries*. New Hyde Park, N.Y.: University Books, 1966.

Frazer, Sir James G., *The Golden Bough*. New York: The Macmillan Co., 1956, in one volume.

Giraldus, Cambrensis, *Itinerary through Wales*. London: 1863.

Graves, Robert, *The White Goddess*. New York: Creative Age Press, 1948.

Halliday, W.R., *Indo-European Folk-Tales and Greek Legend*. Cambridge, England: Cambridge University Press, 1933.

Hansen, Chadwick, *Witchcraft at Salem*. New York: George Braziller, 1969.

Heuvelmans, Bernard, *On the Track of Unknown Animals*. London: Hill & Wang, Paladin Books, 1965.

Homer, *The Odyssey*, trans. by W.H.D. Rouse. New York: Mentor (New American Library), 1964.

Hughes, Pennethorne, *Witchcraft*. Baltimore: Penguin Books, 1967.

Ions, Veronica, *Indian Mythology*. Feltham, England: Paul Hamlyn, 1967.

Kittelsen, Thomas, *Troll i Norge*. Oslo: Forlaget Norsk Kunstreproduksjon, 1968.

The Larousse Encyclopedia of Mythology. London: Paul Hamlyn, 1959.

Lys, Claudia de, *A Treasury of Superstitions*. New York: Philosophical Library, 1957.

MacCana, Proinsias, *Celtic Mythology*. Feltham, England: Paul Hamlyn, 1970.

160

Bibliography

Mandeville, Sir John de, *Mandeville's Travels*, ed. by E. C. Seymour. London: Oxford University Press, 1968.

McCulloch, Florence, *Mediaeval Latin and French Bestiaries*. Chapel Hill, N.C.: University of North Carolina Press, 1960.

Michelet, Jules, *Satanism and Witchcraft*. New York: Citadel Press, 1939.

Middleton, John, ed., *Magic, Witchcraft and Curing*. Garden City, N.Y.: The Natural History Press, 1967.

Osborne, Harold, *South American Mythology*. Feltham, England: Paul Hamlyn, 1968.

Parrinder, Geoffrey, *African Mythology*. Feltham, England: Paul Hamlyn, 1967.

Raffel, Burton, trans., *Beowulf*. New York: Mentor (New American Library), 1963.

Robbins, Rossell Hope, *The Encyclopedia of Witchcraft and Demonology*. New York: Crown Publishers, 1959.

Ross, Anne, *Pagan Celtic Britain*. New York: Columbia University Press, 1967.

S.M.C. of the Dominican Congregation of St. Catherine of Siena, *Once in Cornwall*. New York: Longmans, Green and Co., 1944.

Sanderson, Ivan T., *Abominable Snowmen*. Philadelphia: Chilton Books Co., 1961.

Seznec, Jean, *The Survival of the Pagan Gods*. New York: Harper Torchbooks, 1953.

Spence, Lewis, *An Encyclopedia of Occultism*. New Hyde Park, N.Y.: University Books, 1968.

Summers, Montague, *The Werewolf*. New Hyde Park, N.Y.: University Books, 1966.

Thompson, Stith, *The Folktale*. New York: Dryden Press, 1951.

Thomson, David, *The People of the Sea.* London: Turnstile Press, 1954.

Tolkien, J.R.R., "Tree and Leaf." *The Tolkien Reader,* New York: Ballantine Books, 1966.

Tracey, Hugh, *The Lion on the Path.* New York: Frederick A. Praeger, 1967.

White, T.H., *The Bestiary: A Book of Beasts.* New York: Capricorn Books, 1960.

INDEX

Page references for illustrations are in italic type.

Abominable Snowman, 23
Adramelech, 81
Africa, 19, 62, 65, 69, 71, 75, 116,
    123, 129, 138, 141, 156
Afrit, the, 76
Agares, Devil, 81
Agogwe, the, 69, *70*, 71
Alaska, 92
Algeria, 21
Amazon, the, 71
Amon, 81, 82
Angels, the, 88, *91*, 113
  Hierarchies of, 89–90
Angiras, the, 88
Animals. *See* Halfway People
Apprentice, Sorcerer's, 95
Apsaras, the, 108, 132
Arab Countries, 75, 76
Asia, 9, 65
Assyria, 88
Astaroth, 81, 82
Australia, 92
Australopithecus, 69, 71

Baal, 81, 82
baboons, 117, 120, 122-123

Bael, 81
Balan, 81
Banshee, 84–85
Barnum, P.T., 66, 154
Beelzebub, 81
Beowulf, 13–14
Bes, 62, 66
Big Heads, 120
Big People. *See* Giants
Black Annis, 84
Bloody Bones, 86, *87*
Blue Men of the Minch, 145–146,
    147
Bodach, 86
Boggarts, 50, 86
Bogie, 86
Bogle-bo, 86
Bogles, 50, 86
British Isles, 9, 20, 34, 36, 38, 52, 108
Brittany, 28
Browne, Sir Thomas, 153
Brownies, 42, 47–50, 56, 82
  cleaning house, *49*
Brown Man of the Moors, 86
Bucca, 86
Bugaboo, 86

163

Bugbear, 86

Cailleach Bheur, 84
Caribbean Islands, 92
Canada, 92
Celtic Myths, 28, 37, 38-43, 84, 86
Centaurs, 106, 108, 110
  on a mountain, 107
Central America, 60, 106
Ceylon, 71, 153, 156
changelings, 33–34, 42–43
Chile, 114
Chemosit, the, 75
Cherruve, the, 114
China, 10, 21, 78, 123
Chiron, 108
Christianity, 4, 55, 97, 98
Church, the, 97, 100, 138, 151
Cornwall, 28, 47, 48, 51, 59, 149, 159
Corrigans, 52
Cottingley Fairies, 72–73
covens, 101
Crete, 111–112
Cyclopes, 1, 2, 7–8

Demonology, 80
Demons, ix, 75–76, 78, 82, 109
  possession by, 95, 125, 127, 134
Denmark, 153, 154
Devil, the, 79, 80, 98, 99, 134

pacts with, 100, 125, 142
worshipers of, 100
Devil Kings, 80–81
Devils, 75, 78–80, 90, 109
  chief, 81
  Chinese, 78
  number of, 81
Devon, 28, 51, 116
Djinn, 75–76
  in a bottle, 77
Dobie, the, 50
Dog-headed Men, 115–116
Domania, 53, 55
Domovoi, 53, 55
Doyle, Sir Arthur Conan, 73
Dracs, the, 141
Dragons, 14
Druids, 40–41
Dryads, 85–86, 136
dugong, a, 155, 156
Dvorovoi, 55
Dwarfs, real, 66
Dwarfs, 5, 57–63
  legendary vs. real, 66

East Indies, 92
Eeyeekalduk, 60
Egypt, 65, 117–118
Elijah of Chelm, Rabbi, 10
Elves, 64, 65

England, 5, 7, 9, 31, 43, 47, 56, 59,
    60, 72, 82, 83, 84, 86, 102, 110,
    116, 149
esbats, 101
Eskimo Myths, 60
Europe, 4, 78, 82, 97, 116, 120
    central, 10, 53
    northern, 2, 9, 28
    western, 1, 24, 71

Faery, a, *29*
Faery Folk, 27–46, 51, 97
    dancing at Stonehenge, *39*
    playing with primrose girl, *32*
Faery Godmothers, 43, *45*
Faery Ring, 37, 41
familiar, a, 100
Far East, 116
Fauns, 110
Fiends, 79–80
Fifinellas, 56
Finland, 92
Flat Holme, 20
folktales, origin of, xi–xii
France, 43, 44, 92, 139
Frost Giants, 2, 15
Fuaths, the, 142

Gahongas, 60
Ganconer, the, 35

Gandayaks, 60
Gandharvas, 108, 109, 132
Gardner, Edward L., 72, 73
Gentle Annie, 84
Germany, 21, 53, 82
Gesner, Conrad, 120
Giantesses, special skill of, 5
Giants, ix, 1–2, *3*, 4–14, 15, 18, 20,
    21, 26, 66, 115
    Asian, 9
    Frost, 2, 15
    Iroquois, 9
Giants' Causeway, 20
Glaistig, the, 111
Gnomes, 59
goats, 25, 78, 80, 98 100, 109-111
Goblins, 14, 82–83, 101
gods, 82, 86, 140, 141
goddesses, 84
Golem, the, 10–12
    of Prague, *11*
Gonzales, Peter, 133
Gorgons, 115
Grabbist Giant, 5, *6*, 7, 18, 19
Grant, the, 109
Greece, 2, 4, 5, 8, 85, 98, 106, 108,
    112, 113, 115, 118, 136, 141
Gremlins, 56
Grendel, 13–15, 19
Grendel's Mother, 13, 14

Griffiths, Frances, 72–73

habitats of Impossible People.
hadropithecus, 68–69
Hag, a, 13
   Blue, of Scotland, 84
Hags, 83–84
Halfway People, 105–134
Hallowe'en, 96–97, 101
Hamadryads, 86, 136
Harpies, 113
Hawker, Robert S., 159
Hecatoncheires, 2
Heinzelmännchen, 53
Herakles, 96, 108
Heuvelmans, Dr. Bernard, 68, 69
Hidden People, 44, 46
Hindu Mythology, 76
Hobhole Hob, 48
Hob, the (Hobgoblin), 52–53, 56
Holland, Philemon, 152
Homo sapiens, 20–21, 92
horses, 106-110, 132
Hudson, Geoffrey, 73
Hudson, Hendrik, 153
Hulderfolk, 44
Hydra, the, 96
hypertrichosis, 132–133, 134

Impossible People, origin of, ix–xi,
   74
Imps, 79

India, 9, 76, 82, 88, 92, 116, 122, 132
Indo-European Mythology, 55, 84
Ireland, 28, 35, 37, 46, 52, 84, 108,
   142, 152
Isle of Man, 121

Japan, 60, 157
Java, 21
Jewish myths, 10
Johnson, Samuel, 122
Jotuns, 2, 4, 74

Kalanoro, 67–69
Kappa, 60, 62
Kenya, 21
Kingmingoarkulluk, 60
Knockers, 59
Kotokely, 67
Kobolds, 53, *54*, 82
Krampus, 83

Labyrinth, the, 111–112
Lamassu, the, 88
Lamia, the, 117
Lar, the, 56
lemurs, 68, 116
Leonard, 81
Leow, Rabbi Yehuda, 12
Leprechauns, 52
Leshy, the, 62–63

Index

Liban, 151
Light Elves, 64–65
Little People, 47–73
Lorelei, the, 138, 140
Lutins, 52
lycanthropy, 134

Machnow, 19
Madagascar, 68–69, 115–116
Maes Knoll, 20
Magi, the, 94
Magicians, 90, 92, 93–95, 100
Mandeville, Sir John De, 110, 120,
    121
Mannanan Mac Lir, 121
Manticore, the, 122–123
Mara, 82
maribundas, the, 71
Maruts, 9
May Eve, 37, 101
Medusa, 115
Melusina, 139–140
Mermaids, 113, 141, 146, 148–154,
    156–157, 159
  in Zennor harbor, 150
Mermen, 146, 151, 157
Merrows, the, 145
midgets, 65-66
Midsummer Eve, 37
Minotaur, 111, 112
Moloch, 81, 82

Monopods, 120–121
Muryans, 51
myths, origin of, xi–xii
    See also names of individual
    countries

Nagas, the, 114
Naginis, the, 114
Nandi bear, the, 75
Near East, 82, 88, 118
Necromancers, 95
Nergal, 81
New World, 153
nittaewo, the, 71
Nixes, the, 136, 138
North America, 9, 60, 71, 123, 146
Norway, 16, 44
Nuckelavee, the, 109, 122
Nymphs,
  Forest, 85, 136
    Water, 85, 130, 136, *137*, 138,
    141, 154
    See also Dryads; Hamadryads;
    Oreads

Oannes, 140–141
Odysseus, 7–8
Ogres, 1, 7, 12–15, 21–22, 74
Ohdowas, 60
Olokun, 141
One with the White Hand, 86

orang pendek, 71
Oreads, 85, 136
Ovinnik, 55
Oxen, King of, 10

People of the Sea, 135–159
Persia, 94, 122
Peter of Greece, Prince, 24
Philippine Islands, 65
pithecanthropus, 21–22
Pixies, 42, 50–51
Pliny, 152
Pluto, 81, 82
Poland, 10
Polevik, the, 63
Polo, Marco, 115–116
Polyphemus, 7–8
poltergeist, 50
Pooka, the, 108–109
porphyria, 133, 134
Prague, 10–12
psychic phenomena, 73
pygmies, 65

Ravana, Demon, 78
regions associated with legends and
    myths. *See* names of individual
    countries
Roane, the, 142
Romans, 56
Ruadh, Angus, 144–145

Rumpelstiltskin, 50
Russell, Gerald, 24
Russia, 19, 53, 62, 71, 92, 130

sabbats, 101, 102
Sahara Desert, 92
Saint Collen, 31
Saint Nicholas, 83
sasquatch, 26, 71
Satan, 80, 81
Satyrs, 80, 98, 109–110
Scandinavia, 28, 44, 59, 64, 142
Schliemann, Heinrich, xi
Scotland, 28, 44, 47, 83, 84, 85, 86,
    103, 109, 142, 149, 152, 157
seals, 142-145, 156-157
Sea, People of the, 135–159
second sight, 44, 46
Selchies, the, 142–145, 156
shape-shifters, 105, 123, 129, 130,
    132, 142
Shipton, Eric, 24
Siberia, 92, 130
Sileni, 110
Silent Moving Ones, 42
Sirens, 113-114, 138, 140, 154
Slavic Myths, 53, 62, 142
snakes, 114–115, 117
Sorceress, 92, 94
Sorcerers, 92, 94, 95, 96
South America, 60, 106, 123, 156

Index

Sphynx, the Great, 117–118, *119*
Sphynxes, Greek, 118–120
Spina, Alphonsus de, 81
Steep Holme, 20
Stonehenge, 38, 40–41
    fairylike creatures dancing at, *39*
Stonor, Charles, 24
Stratton, Charles Sherwood, 66
Sumatra, 71
supernatural, the, 93–94
Swan-Maiden, the, 130, *131*, 132
Sweden, 64

Tailed Men, 116–117
Tepictoton, 60
Teutonic myths, 2, 4, 57, 58, 64, 136
Tinkerbelle, Peter Pan's, 65
Titans, 1, 2, 4, 74
Tom Thumb, General, 66
Tom Tit Tot, 50
Tootega, 60, *61*
Transcendant Pig, the, 10
Trewhella, Mathey, 149
Tritons, 141
Trolls, 1, 15–18, 59, 97
    Forest, 15, 16, *17*
    House, 18
    Mountain, 15–16
    River, 15, 16
Tuatha De Danann, 37, 40, 41, 42, 43, 84

Urisks, 110–111

Vampires, 128
Vodyanoi, the, 142

Waddell, Major L. A., 23
Wales, 28, 46
Warlocks, 100
Washer, the, 85
Water Demons, 13
Water Spirit, ix
Wenlock Edge, 20
Werewolf, the, 123–129, 132–134
    and other were-beasts, 123, 129–130
    in the woods, *126*
Weyer, Johan, 81
Widgets, 56
Will o' the Wisp, 42
Witches, 80, 83, 90, 92, 96–98, 100–104
    Male. *See* Warlocks
Wizards, 92, 94
Workers of Evil, 74–104
Wright, Elsie, 72

Yarthkins, 60
Yeats, William Butler, 37, 40, 41
Yeti, 23–26
Ymir, 2, 57

169

ABOUT THE AUTHOR A young New York author and editor, Georgess McHargue cannot remember a time when she did not write. But she does remember that even her earliest efforts centered on imaginary beings—although they were primarily those of her own invention. Georgess McHargue has written seven books for young readers as well as editing *The Best of Both Worlds,* a literary anthology for young adults.

The author was prompted to write THE IMPOSSIBLE PEOPLE because "...most mythology, as told for children, is a hideous bore." She feels that "...the interesting thing about myths is not what they say but why." In the course of research for this book, she traveled widely in Britain visiting Stonehenge, Tintagel, the fairy castle at Glastonbury, and the home of the Grabbist Giant.

ABOUT THE ARTIST Frank Bozzo grew up in New York City where he studied at the School of Visual Arts. He started his career by doing magazine and book illustrations. In 1968, he illustrated his first children's book, coincidentally also the first book by Georgess McHargue, *The Beasts of Never.* Since then, his pictures for such books as *Are You My Friend?, The Fearsome Brat,* and AIGA award-winner, *Herman's Hat,* have gained him wide recognition in the field.

In addition to his artwork, Frank Bozzo also finds time to teach at his alma mater. The artist and his wife make their home in Manhattan.